ABOUT

Marva Tyndale has written a groundbreaking book that will impact generations to come. As a youth pastor, I have had numerous meetings with parents seeking advice on how they can effectively transform their rebellious children and youth. I have used and recommended biblical, psychological and other methods in the past, but finally here is a resource I can recommend that uses divine strategies to restore and engage our young people.

REV. TY JACKSON
FOUNDER, REMNANT MINISTRIES, ONTARIO, CANADA

Keeping Our Hope Alive is a tremendous resource for anyone looking for an ultimate, permanent and divine solution to the epidemic problem in which today's teenagers and young adults are repeatedly finding themselves. Marva Tyndale's insight and teaching gleaned from God's Word is an effective prescription for parents to discover victory and restore relationship with their children. It is a tool for finding victory in the midst of struggle and pain.

REV. MIKE VAN SLINGERLAND
EXECUTIVE DIRECTOR, FREEDOM VILLAGE OF CANADA

As a father and pastor I have found the strategies in the book to be relevant for all people who love their family and friends and are in need of practical yet effective tools—tools that work! Marva Tyndale has tag teamed with the Holy Spirit to write a must-read in the Kingdom of God.

REV. DWIGHT RICHARDS
CO-FOUNDER, WALKING IN WHOLENESS MINISTRIES, ONTARIO, CANADA

Pastors and other church leaders across the nations have long awaited a practical Bible-based resource like this to help families with troubled youth. In recent years even the government has been looking to the church for answers to the youth crisis in various communities. Now, with this resource guide to divine intervention strategies, Marva Tyndale has given to the church a practical tool that will inspire hope and produce results. I encourage leaders to get *Keeping Our Hope Alive* into the hands of the people and train them how to use it."

DR. RAYMOND CRADOCK PH.D D.TH
THE BROADCAST GROUP, UK AND USA

In this book Marva Tyndale offers many practical suggestions and strategies for parents whose children have strayed from God's path for their lives. The Bible tells us that our faith and love spring from the hope that is within us (Colossians 1:4-5). Maintaining hope is therefore essential in order to exercise faith and love during difficult times. *Keeping Our Hope Alive* ought to do just what the title says for parents and others with youth in crisis.

REV. TERRY BONE
CO-FOUNDER, IDENTITY AND DESTINY MINISTRIES, ONTARIO, CANADA

I will never forget an honest father-son exchange with my big boy when he said to me, "Dad, if two people are going to heaven it's you and Mom, but as for me, I want to be left alone to decide where I want to go."

While respecting his request, his mother and I purposed in our hearts to continue loving him and never lose hope. In spite of his numerous wrong decisions, years later by God's grace we saw him respond to an appeal to refocus on Christ: the Way, the Truth and the Life.

Marva Tyndale's *Keeping Our Hope Alive,* crafted from her own struggle, is practical help that assures us first of all that we are not alone in the struggle for our children's salvation; secondly, that certain biblical strategies can effectively replace our helplessness; and thirdly, that keeping hope alive begins with ourselves.

Keeping Our Hope Alive is an important key in the restoration of our wayward children, but its right use may not come easily for many well-intentioned, hurting parents. May the Holy Spirit use our labor of love and ultimately cause us to see our precious sons and daughters restored.

REV. DENNIS E. WHITE
SENIOR PASTOR, ISLINGTON EVANGEL CENTRE
ONTARIO, CANADA

KEEPING OUR HOPE ALIVE

Myndale

JAN. 14. 2012.

For speaking engagements and ministry information, you may contact the author at:

REAL IDENTITY DISCOVERY MINISTRIES
Box 29622-377 Burnhamthorpe Road East
Mississauga, Ontario L5A 4H2
Canada

416-277-6891
info@realidteaching.org

www.realidteaching.org
www.keepingourhopealive.org

KEEPING OUR HOPE ALIVE

Strategies to Restore
Teens and Young Adults

MARVA M. TYNDALE

VMI Publishers • Sisters, Oregon

Keeping Our Hope Alive:
Strategies to Restore Teens and Young Adults

All Scripture quotations, unless otherwise indicated, are taken from the *New International Version of the Bible.* Copyright © 1973, 1978, 1984, by the International Bible Society. Used by permission.

Scripture quotations marked NLT are taken from the *Holy Bible, New Living Translation,* copyright 1996, 2004. Used by permission of Tyndale House Publishers, Inc., Wheaton, Illinois 60189. All rights reserved.

Scripture quotations marked AMP are taken from *The Amplified Bible.* Copyright 1987. Used by permission of The Lockman Foundation, La Habra, California. All rights reserved.

Scripture quotations marked KJV are taken from the *King James Version.* Public Domain.

Scripture quotations marked NASB are taken from the New American Standard Bible. Copyright 1995. Used by permission of The Lockman Foundation, La Habra, California. All rights reserved.

Published by
VMI Publishers
Sisters, Oregon
www.vmipublishers.com

ISBN: 1-933204-68-0
ISBN: 13: 978-1-933204-68-0
Library of Congress Control Number: 2008933068

Printed in the USA.

Cover design by Joe Bailen

DEDICATION

To God's Hopekeeper Warriors everywhere
who dare to become part of the solution in restoring a
generation of young people.

CONTENTS

Foreword

Keeping Our Hope Alive is more than a resource guide. A Warriors' Handbook—that's what it is! As a wife, mother, grandmother and co-pastor of an inner city church, I say this book needs to be in the hands of every woman who wants the tools with which to impact the next generation, especially the lives of those she touches. Whether you think or feel like a warrior on the front lines or not, the reality is that every woman is a warrior, and this book puts powerful weapons in our hands.

But this handbook is not just for women and mothers. It is for men and fathers too! It is very much about us fighting together for our kids, at any and every age, for their friends and for others around who may not have anyone else praying for them. But if you are not a parent, it is still for you. It is for anyone who has a heart to see prodigals return home and a generation of lost youth restored.

The key strategies and tactics woven throughout this book are like secret weapons that can be used by anyone. They will help us all to stand strong, pray through and be the victorious Christians we were meant to be. Then as God's Hopekeeper Warriors we can go on to restore, strengthen, and empower the next generation.

If my mom were still alive she would have loved this book. She stood for me in dark times. When I was involved in an outlaw bikers' gang for nine years, she prayed me back to God. My mom did not have a ministry in the public eye, but she had calluses on her knees. I am the woman I am today because of the powerful prayers of a tenacious mother.

At a meeting with Tracy Stewart, I heard her tell a story that I would like to share with you. Her friend was visiting her little granddaughter and asked, "Where's Daddy?" to which she replied, "Grama, he workin'."

"Well, where's he workin'?" she asked.

"I don't know Grama, but he workin'."

The Grandmother persisted in her questioning, "When is he coming home?"

Again the same response, "I don't know Grama, he workin'."

Then the revelation came. We might not be able to see presently just what our heavenly Father is doing, but when the enemy attacks, when the doubts come, when we can't see clearly, our determined response needs to be: "He Workin'!"

You see, our Father in heaven is at work—in our lives, our ministries, our homes and in our children's lives, even when we can't see it. In the words of Jesus, "My Father is always at his work to this very day, and I, too, am working" (John 5:17).

We all need to learn how to trust even when we can't trace. Keeping Our Hope Alive will undoubtedly take you to new levels of knowledge and faith. Get ready for an impartation of fresh faith, hope and love as you read, study and put into practice these useful and practical tools.

JOY CLARKE

PASTOR, THE JOSHUA CENTER &

CO-FOUNDER THE HAMILTON DREAM CENTER

THE TESTIMONY OF
ONE YOUNG MAN'S JOURNEY TO RESTORATION

I am thoroughly convinced that had it not been for the saving grace of the Lord Jesus Christ that rescued me from anger, alcohol and drugs I would still be lost in confusion and hopelessness today. And because of what I have experienced, I can say with full assurance that this same restoration is possible for other young men and women that have gone astray.

For many young people, heaven and hell, God and Satan, and even absolute truth are debatable subjects. But the reality that I live every day is that they do exist and impact our lives whether or not we choose to believe. An even bigger reality that I have come to understand is that God has a plan for each life, and that Satan and his evil forces will do everything in their power to stop it.

While we are each accountable for the choices we make in life, I believe that Satan's evil intent to sabotage God's purposes on the earth is the bottom-line reason for the crisis that I and many other youths have faced. It is the reason for the crisis that increasing numbers of youths are still facing, and the reason for the struggles that many will contend with in the future.

I did not always understand that God had a plan for my life, and I still don't know how big His plans are for me. But what I now realize is that Satan has been trying real hard to stop me from fulfilling God's purpose for my life.

My life battles started shortly after birth when at ten days old I was struck with a high fever of unknown origin that kept me hospitalized for several days. Then at three months, I was diagnosed with what is known in the medical field as a "stridor," caused by an abscess (a retropharyngeal abscess) in the back of my throat that obstructed my breathing. But what the enemy meant for evil, God turned for good. God delivered and healed me, but not before He used the trying times to gain another great victory: my mother's salvation. During my two months of hospitalization, my mother had grown close to some of the nursing staff and, as a result of what she observed in the life of one key nurse, was drawn to Jesus Christ and accepted Him as her personal Savior.

No one knew then that out of my near-death infant illnesses God was equipping my mother with what she would need to bring me through a later life-threatening battle with anger, drugs and alcohol.

I had grown up in the church as a child, knowing many Bible stories and even being able to recite the Beatitudes. But I questioned it all during my adolescent years, for it seemed that my circumstances contradicted every Sunday school lesson I had ever heard about the love of Christ.

My twelve-year-old mind could not understand how it is that God had sent His only Son to save mankind yet had taken my father. Furthermore, I failed to comprehend how a simple accident of two broken arms could lead to a fatal blood clot that took my father's life six weeks after. I didn't know where to find the love of God the Father that was preached about week after week while my dear father was now "resting in peace." I became very confused, and because I found no answers my confusion quickly turned to anger and hatred.

Recognizing the state I was in, my mother decided it would be best for me to spend my high school years in a Christian environment. I appreciated the sacrifice she made, for grades nine through eleven were some of the best years of my life. I developed great friendships and it seemed for a while that I would not have to confront my anger or any of the other issues of the past.

I later learnt, however, that no matter how far we run from our problems, they will always catch up with us because they are still ours to deal with. Sure enough, my anger tracked me down and slowly beat me to a pulp at the end of my junior year.

Trying to cope, I started with one cigarette, then a joint. Then, before I knew it I found myself getting drunk or high at every opportunity. Because of my school's zero tolerance policy and the appreciation I still had for the sacrifice my mother had made, I was able for a while to contain my activities to weekends. By the time my senior year rolled around, my life had become one big façade and ugly charade. I had mastered the art of doing everything to please the people around me so as not to raise any suspicions.

Graduation brought a much-needed relief. That day as I hugged my older brother down the walk, I was filled with what felt like joy that I would no longer have to live a lie. This was my chance to cut loose and do my own thing. That summer I plunged fully into alcoholism and drug abuse. Devastating results followed quickly. I lost an awesome relationship with a girl, destroyed many bridges with good friends and found myself with no one to depend on.

But this was exactly where God wanted me to be. After smoking up one night, I somehow realized my hopelessness, saw the severity of my situation and decided that I needed help.

It was indeed for such a time as this that God had helped my mother to find salvation and relationship with Jesus. Through this awful time of my life, my mother's hope-filled passion and determination for God to turn my life around drove her into fervent prayer and fasting. She found God's path of victory for me and successfully guided me to Freedom Village U.S.A.

On January 3, 2006 I enrolled in the program. Freedom Village became home and my lifeline to victory. Upon arriving there, the first thing that struck me was the genuine contentment I saw in just about everyone. They had the kind of joy that I was lacking, something that I had missed even during those years of growing up in the church. It didn't take me long to discover the secret, and I knew that I had to hand over my life to Jesus Christ. I made the decision to accept Christ as my personal Savior, fully aware that there would be struggles along this new path, and that I would be tested and tried. But I was sure of one thing: I now had someone, Christ Himself, to rely on with His sustaining strength and grace.

It was only a year after being restored to new life in Christ that God entrusted me with a test—not for His sake but for mine. It was an opportunity for me to see the extent to which my heart was changed. My older sister whom I loved very much, Paulanne Hoskins, was diagnosed with Osteo-Sarcoma (the same cancer as Terry Fox). She died on March 1, 2007, a few weeks after her twenty-second birthday. The pain seemed unbearable because I had not only lost a sibling, I had lost an amazing friend. This time around, however, the trust I had gained in Christ and the love I had found in Him carried me through the pain and saved me from the anger and confusion that had almost destroyed me at my father's death.

God has been so amazing to me, and in this new season of my life I continue looking to Him for direction in all areas, and for His grace to keep me from the evils of my past. I cling tenaciously to the hope and promise of a future at the center of His will. He has given me all the tools I need, the people to encourage and support me, and above all a passion for those who are lost and hurt. I praise the Lord for His unfailing love that never gave up on me, for His salvation, and for making my life a true success.

When I think of how fast I had been traveling on the slippery road to destruction, I know that the fervent prayers of my mother and others were the key to my restoration. Their prayers released a mighty move of God in my life that I could not resist. Their prayers prepared my heart to receive help; prepared a welcoming place for me in the Freedom Village family where I found Christ; and sustained me through the program as I grew closer to the Lord and experienced His transforming power day by day. Their prayers were like wings that carried me over on the other side to victory in Christ.

In Christ I have found the greatest love mankind has ever known, and it has brought me victory over drugs, alcohol, and other destructive forces. I believe with all my heart that with the prayers and relentless hope of parents and others, youth in crisis, pain and rebellion can experience this same victory.

That's why I thank God for a book like this. It will help parents and others to keep alive their hope of restoration and pray troubled young people through to victory. I believe God will use it as a tool to restore and transform generations of young people now and in the future. May God bless all who give of themselves for the fulfillment of God's purpose in the lives of young men and women.

ADAM HOSKINS

TORONTO, CANADA

FREEDOM VILLAGE U.S.A. ALUMNI (2007)

ACKNOWLEDGMENTS

With special thanks…

To my heavenly Father whose gift of life and unconditional love are my greatest treasures. To Jesus who has satisfied all the deep longings of my heart and made me complete. To the Holy Spirit for teaching me and patiently helping me to become all that I am called to be.

To my husband, Maurice, for believing in me and in the vision God has given me. I thank God for you and for what our thirty-one years of marriage have helped us to become.

To my four precious children, Tommy, Margo, Jonathan, and David, who together have put me through over twenty-nine years of "parenting school," a process that God has used to birth supernatural hope in me. I thank God for each of you and wouldn't trade you for the world!

To my wonderful grandchildren, Shadya, Tahjay, Tariq, Isaiah, Unique Joy, Javion, and others yet to be born—my hope for you is boundless. Thank you for adding the honor of "grand" to my life's work.

To Pastor Joy Clarke and "Pastor-in-training" Adam Hoskins, two of God's chosen witnesses and living proof of His faithfulness in restoring lives. Adam, you are the answer to every parent's hope! Thank you both for sowing your life experiences into this work to bless others.

To the many pastors and leaders who have shepherded, encouraged, and mentored me over the years, seeing more in me than I at first had eyes to see. To Terry Bone, Raymond Cradock, Ty Jackson, Dwight Richards, Mike Van Slingerland, and Dennis White, thank you for the time you invested to read and endorse the book.

To my first covenant and financial partner, Gwendolyn Houston, one to whom God has given the gift of language and through whom His generosity flows. Your labor of love in editing the many drafts of the manuscript will never be lost or forgotten.

To my Hopekeeper partners, Rose Watson, Rhonda McLeod, and Pauline Hoskins, whose vision and anointing have enriched my life, my ministry and this project.

To my prayer partners for the many hours of prayer they have invested in my ministry, in my family, and in my life.

To Inez and David Ayres and to Pamela and Andrew Smith for their faithful support, as well as my other ministry partners, associates, and friends whose participation in the ministry continues to encourage me. I appreciate you more than words can say.

To Bill Carmichael of VMI Publishers and the team that worked alongside me to put the finishing touches and stamp of excellence on my work. Your support has been invaluable.

Introduction

I settled down with my friend, the mother of two young adults, at a small table for two off to the side in our busy neighborhood coffee shop. It was one of our "staying-in-touch" meetings that usually doubled as a discipleship session because of my friend's eager desire to grow spiritually.

On this occasion, however, the atmosphere was somewhat different, for we both seemed to have had other things on our minds. Eventually, our conversation got to the subject of the desperation of parents who do not know what to do about their grown children that are headed for disaster or are there already.

We had been talking for about an hour when my friend leaned back in her chair and threw her arms in the air.

"Can somebody tell me what's really going on? They've all gone crazy, and I do not understand." She paused, placed both hands on her forehead then continued. "Can't we just round them all up, whip them off to some remote place, and teach them some sense?

"If only it were that simple." I chuckled. "We wouldn't get very far. You know that. And teaching will not help either. Not at this stage anyway. It is going to take much more than that. Want to know what I really think?"

She raised her eyebrows, inviting me to continue.

"It is going to take divine intervention." I paused, expecting a response, but she did not say a word. She just raised her eyebrows higher. "They've been blinded. There's a veil over their minds and eyes. That veil first has to

19

be removed before they can receive the truth and begin to change. Only the power of Jesus Christ in their lives can change them. But believe it or not, we hold the key."

"What is *that* supposed to mean? Are you saying that we are responsible?"

"Not at all. But there's something that we can do. We have what it takes. We may find it hard to reach them directly at first, but we can use strategies that will pave the way for God to do what only He can do—change their hearts."

"Pave the way?" she muttered.

"Yes," I replied with strong conviction. "Pave the way for God to intervene in their lives. We can make a difference if we'd cooperate with God."

After giving my friend a brief explanation of what divine intervention was all about, with a sight of relief, she said, "So there *is* hope after all?"

Becoming Part of the Solution

By the end of our conversation, my friend had come to the realization that she wasn't as helpless as she had thought. She could in fact be part of the solution.

How about you? If you have any concern whatsoever for the plight of our young people, you are a Hopekeeper candidate—one who will keep hope alive for God to intervene in their lives, deliver them, and restore them to a purposeful life. You may not be a parent with a teen or young adult at risk, but it doesn't matter. You can still be part of the solution.

The harsh reality is that many young people who attempt suicide or turn to crime, drugs, prostitution, gangs, and other destructive lifestyles have been abandoned by their families. They need someone to love them enough to fight for their restoration. Can God count on you to stand in the gap on their behalf? (See Ezekiel 22:30.)

Our availability to be used by God, our sincere desire and willingness to cooperate with Him are all that is required to get started. It is not too late for this generation of young people. The God for whom nothing is impossible is well able to restore them.

Introduction

Having filled me with His supernatural hope over many years of trying circumstances with my own grown children, the Lord has commissioned me to share His hope with hurting parents and others who are seeking solutions to help restore this generation of young people that is in crisis.

If you are one of those hurting parents, I do not believe that this book has come to you by chance. There is no such thing as coincidence. I believe that by His sovereign design, the Lord has brought it to you because He has heard the cry of your heart. He wants you to know that He identifies fully with your pain.

Also, as parents, we cannot forget that God, our heavenly Father, is the first parent whose grown children (Adam and Eve) rebelled and fell into the crisis of sin that damaged themselves and the entire human race. So God truly understands and knows our sorrow. But the most encouraging part of all is that He has all power to heal our broken hearts and restore the lives of our offspring. In God's redemption of humanity through His Son, Jesus Christ, there is provision for the restoration of each of our sons and daughters and for other young people as well.

If you are not a parent, but you have a strong desire to see young people restored out of crisis, I believe that this desire did not originate with you. It came from God. Whether you are a relative, a family friend, a pastor, a youth worker, a counselor, a mentor, a member of the church, a rehabilitation service provider, or a member of the community at large, you have in a sense been chosen or called by God to be one of His Hopekeepers. Not only has He chosen or called you as a Hopekeeper, God has equipped you with whatever you need to make a difference in the life of some teenager or young adult. This resource has not come to you by chance either. In it you will find hope, insights, and the help you need to become part of God's solution for our young people's restoration.

May we together become a mighty army of Hopekeepers who will do what it takes to see the God of hope restore our generation of teens and young adults that are in trouble or headed for trouble.

How to Get the Most from This Guide

Keeping Our Hope Alive is a resource guide. It is not just for information purposes or casual reading. It is for application, and it will require some work and commitment on your part to implement the strategies that are presented. I encourage you to make the investment, for it will be well worth it.

Our concept of work is that it involves toiling. However, the work that these strategies require is the kind of work that God did at creation. You will be putting your words to work for you. You will be using words to release your faith and create the reality that God intended for our young people.

The strategies are not magical formulas, so as you persevere in applying them, keep in mind what God promises: "Let us not become weary in doing good, for at the proper time we will reap a harvest if we do not give up" (Galatians 6:9).

To make it easier for you to use this guide, we have divided it into two parts. Part I lays the foundation, and Part II documents divine intervention strategies with examples for you to apply. We have also included an index to assist you in researching different topics.

The following guidelines will help you achieve maximum benefit from the strategies.

1. Pray and ask for the Holy Spirit to guide you as you read through each chapter. *Keeping Our Hope Alive* is based on biblical wisdom and principles, not on the wisdom of the world. Since the Holy Spirit inspired those who wrote the Bible, He is the best person to help you understand and apply its principles.
2. Read through all of Part I before you go on to Part II.
3. Read through Part II more than once. The goal is for the prayers, declarations, decrees and other strategies to become so much a part of you that you will apply them spontaneously. You want the words of hope to be rooted in your heart so that you will have something to draw on at all times, especially when going through extraordinarily difficult seasons.

4. Take the time at the end of each chapter to do the reinforcement exercises.

5. Keep a Hope Journal. Use it to make notes as you read, to record additional prayers, Scriptures, and insights for battle strategies. Also use it to keep track of your victories, no matter how small.

6. Speak audibly when applying the strategies. It will increase their effectiveness.

7. Apply the strategies in an attitude of faith. Expect results.

8. Personalize the material by inserting specific names as much as possible. You will notice that we use the words children, offspring, seed, descendants, teens, young adults, and young people inter-changeably. The book is written primarily for parents, but it is easily adaptable for use by others.

9. Although the book focuses mainly on grown children, the mate-rial can be easily adapted for children of any age group. Reactive or remedial parenting is not God's ideal; so, with God's help, we want to avert the crisis into which many older children have fallen. Where infants and even unborn children are concerned, we have the opportunity to safeguard them through preventa-tive strategies. The last chapter of the book is dedicated to that purpose.

10. Pull out this resource often—not only when you are dealing with situations concerning your own teenager or young adult. Use it to do battle for other young people as well, and continue using it as reinforcement even after your victories have been won.

11. The strategies can be applied generally as well by those whom God would use as intercessors to target particular segments of the teenage and young adult population. For example, those in a particular community or region, those that are behind bars, those struggling with drug addictions, or those involved with gangs and gun violence.

12. Create your own community of hope by joining forces with others and working through the strategies together. "Iron sharpens iron" (Proverbs 27:17).

And be sure to tell others about this resource so that they too can learn how to keep their hope alive.

May God richly bless you with invincible, supernatural hope.

PART I
THE CRISIS AND THE SOLUTION

"And he will [himself] go before Him in the spirit and power of Elijah, to turn back the hearts of the fathers to the children, and the disobedient and incredulous and unpersuadable to the wisdom of the upright [which is the knowledge and holy love of the will of God]—in order to make ready for the Lord a people [perfectly] prepared [in spirit, adjusted and disposed and placed in the right moral state]." (Luke 1:17 AMP)

Chapter One

No Ordinary Kind of Intervention

There are different faces to the crisis into which many of our teens and young adults have fallen. Among other things, the dictionary defines crisis as "a time or state of danger." What is considered a crisis or cause for concern for one person may not be for another. Still, we cannot deny that many of our young people are in great danger and desperately in need of help. It is also alarming that many are beginning to fall into crisis at much younger ages, even before reaching the teen years.

For some the crisis may involve rebellion against parental and other authority, rejection of their faith in Jesus Christ, inner turmoil resulting from abandonment or childhood physical, emotional or sexual abuse, or it may involve experimentation and searching for a sense of identity. For others, the crisis may involve a struggle with emotional issues, substance abuse or addiction, trouble with the law, violence, immorality, or involvement in illegal activities.

Regardless of the face of the crisis, families are hurting everywhere. Escalating violence and murders among young people have thrown many communities into turmoil. Government agencies and law enforcers are searching desperately for answers. In the meantime, many parents are sinking in despair and the worst part of it all is that the majority do not know what to do. But I bring good news. All hope is not lost!

Interestingly enough, this book was inspired not so much by the crisis in our young people's lives but by God's vision of hope for them. So this book is more about our hope for their restoration than it is about their crisis. It is a book about how to keep that hope alive, and how we will see our hope transformed into victory.

It Calls for Divine Intervention

The crisis that our young people are facing calls for intervention beyond the natural or ordinary. Now that they are grown, we have lost much of the opportunity of the earlier years to directly intervene in their lives. We see their lives spinning out of control and we become desperate to get them back on track. However, we quickly realize that in and of ourselves we lack the knowledge and the power to make things right. Sooner or later we recognize that the nature of their crisis calls for divine intervention.

The basic premise underlying divine intervention is our dependency on God.

The basic premise underlying divine intervention is our dependency on God. This dependency acknowledges that we attain victory in the battles of life not by our own natural might and power but by the Spirit of the Lord. "'Not by might nor by power, but by my Spirit,' says the LORD Almighty" (Zechariah 4:6).

Well, what is divine intervention? Divine intervention is God's grace, which is His divine ability, power, favor, and love, working to improve situations and produce lasting change in an individual's heart and life through relationship with Jesus Christ.

Divine intervention operates through a covenant partnership. A covenant in Bible terms is more than a legal agreement. It is a binding obligation or promise in which God says He will do His part if we will do ours. God is a covenant-keeping God. He never breaks covenant, and even when we do, He waits for us to return and honor our part so that He can honor His.

In this covenant partnership we, as God's representatives on earth, give Him the legal access He needs to act on the earth. In turn, He intervenes on our behalf and becomes actively engaged in our affairs.

You may be thinking *God has need of nothing. And He certainly doesn't need permission from anyone to do anything. After all, He is God, the all power-ful Creator.* That is true. But there is a vital principle concerning God's oper-ation in the earth about which we need to be aware.

At creation, God delegated to his human offspring the dominion man-date and authority to rule the earth. In so doing He chose to limit His capac-ity to operate in the earth. Since God operates by principles and will not violate His own laws, He requires the agreement and cooperation of a human agent in order for Him to carry out whatever He desires to do in the earth. (See Genesis 1:28; Psalm 115:16; Matthew 16:19-20.)

Principles of Divine Intervention

Divine intervention involves these six principles:

1. Engaging God, His attributes and weapons in our battles.
2. God contending with spiritual forces of wickedness on our behalf. (See Isaiah 49:25.)
3. God expressing His supernatural ability and attributes through us.
4. Giving priority to God's superior ways and thoughts that may even be considered foolishness to the world. (See Isaiah 55:8; 1 Corinthians 1:20-29.)
5. Exercising the authority we have in Christ to rule in the spiritual realm as kings who proclaim and establish heaven's purposes on the earth.
6. Cooperating with God to influence the spiritual or supernatu-ral realm by our actions taken in the physical or natural realm.

When we speak of the supernatural or spiritual we are not referring to mystical or psychic powers, or to the occult world. We are speaking of the unseen yet real realm of the spirit that is eternal, outside and beyond the physical realm. It is the invisible atmosphere in which spiritual forces oper-ate. This realm is often referred to in the Scriptures as the heavenlies.

As human beings created in God's image, each of us has been designed with a spirit, soul, and body. God's intent was that we would live in the physical realm but influence both the spiritual (unseen) and the physical (visible) realms. However, when Adam and Eve sinned, humanity lost the spiritual authority and power to operate in and influence the unseen realm. Our spiritual authority is restored through faith in Jesus Christ, but there remains in us the tendency to concentrate on and operate from the natural perspective only.

So when it comes to the crisis in our young people's lives, we tend to think of it first from the visible or natural standpoint. We react to it, try to understand it, and confront it on the basis of what we see and hear in the natural. But the Scriptures advocate a different approach: "So we fix our eyes not on what is seen, but on what is unseen. For what is seen is temporary, but what is unseen is eternal" (2 Corinthians 4:18).

We initiate our confrontation of the problem in the spiritual realm.

What are we to do then about our young people's crisis? Do we ignore the visible signs of crisis? Do we cast aside practical or natural solutions? By no means!

Rather, we start with the realization that there is both a spiritual and a natural dimension to their crisis. We seek to understand both dimensions, but we initiate our confrontation of the problem in the spiritual realm. The crisis originated in the spiritual realm, and it is here that real or effective change will take place. We have to start in the spiritual realm if we want lasting change—change that is eternal and not merely temporary.

The Advantages of Divine Intervention

Divine intervention is not an option. It is essential for the resolution of this crisis because it gives us some definite advantages.

- It is through divine intervention that we will receive the wisdom of God to know the practical steps that we must take in the natural.
- Only through divine intervention strategies will the strongholds

of Satan that are keeping our young people in rebellion, addictions, and other forms of bondage be destroyed.

- It is through divine intervention that we first take authority over the hindering spiritual forces of darkness so that our young people can open their hearts to receive God's grace and make choices that will lead to their restoration.

- It is divine intervention that will bring our young people into a personal relationship with Jesus Christ who, according to 1 Corinthians 1:24, is the power of God. This is the only power by which their lives can be rescued, restored and transformed.

It is important to keep in mind that divine intervention strategies do not replace the need for disciplinary action or other forms of direct intervention. Discipline is actually an indispensable hope strategy. "Discipline your son, for in that there is hope; do not be a willing party to his death" (Proverbs 19:18). As God our heavenly Father disciplines us, so He requires that we discipline the children He has entrusted to us.

Divine intervention strategies are not a last resort either. Rather, they ought to be our first response as well as our ongoing course of action. They are both precursory and complementary. They are essential for increasing the effectiveness of natural forms of intervention.

Natural and Divine Intervention at Work

I rarely sit down to watch television shows, but recently I was captivated by an A&E episode of Intervention™ dealing with crystal meth addiction. Many of the scenes were hard on my emotions, and I was greatly relieved at the end when the featured young woman in her late teens agreed to enter a rehabilitation facility.

It was fascinating to see a well orchestrated natural intervention process at work, but the most spectacular thing about this case was the family's hope and faith in God. The prayers said on behalf of the young woman and the involvement of the family's pastor demonstrated a powerful combination of natural and divine intervention strategies. Although I knew nothing about the type of program this young lady was about to enter, the fact that she belonged to a praying family gave me much hope for her successful rehabilitation.

The expression "Prayer changes things" is more than a cliché. Prayer is actually one of the most powerful divine intervention strategies for bringing about change in an individual's heart. It supernaturally transforms the atmosphere of a person's life both within and without by releasing the power of God to work on his/her behalf.

Christ-centered residential rehabilitation programs for young people offer a unique advantage. I believe that their reliance on prayer and other forms of divine intervention to bring their young people into relationship with Christ is the secret to their proven success.[1]

Change must occur at the heart level in order to be sustained, and only through faith in Christ can one experience this kind of change.

Earlier you read the testimony of Adam Hoskins who graduated from Freedom Village. Adam experienced a true change of heart while in the program because of the prayers of his mother, family and friends, and the way the program helped him to nurture a strong personal relationship with Christ. Change must occur at the heart level in order to be sustained, and only through faith in Christ can one experience this kind of change.

I was speaking with a young man recently about a program he was considering for his alcohol abuse. He had attended one introductory meeting but did not return, and I had drawn my own conclusions as to why he had not continued. His explanation sounded like a cop-out, but eventually I was able to perceive something of God's wisdom.

The young man said he did not continue because he was not about to replace one form of addiction with another. He wanted total freedom not a substitute or a crutch. He shared his observation that many of the program participants had exchanged the alcohol for another substance or drug, nicotine and caffeine being the most obvious. At first I defended their approach, saying that this is the path that works for them and at least they were trying. But the wisdom of God broke through my human reasoning.

The only way to truly overcome addiction is by a power greater than the addiction. That power is the Spirit of Christ Himself indwelling the human life by faith. It is misleading to think that just any "higher power" will do. You see, as human beings we were made to live by the power of God that dwells in Christ. "For God was pleased to have all his fullness dwell in him. For in Christ all the fullness of the Deity lives in bodily form" (Colossians 1:19; 2:9). "For in him we live and move and have our being" (Acts 17:28).

The young man was not yet conscious of it, but He was seeking this ultimate power and was not prepared to settle for substitutes. I believe that the advantage Christ-centered and faith-based rehabilitation services offer is that they guide young people to that ultimate power source and help them to sustain their newfound freedom in Christ.

I believe the hand of God is at work divinely guiding this young man to the only source of true freedom. Presently he is at an in-between place, but I believe with all my heart that God will, by the best means possible, help him in due season to come fully into the light and break free.

God's Word cannot lie: "For everyone who asks receives; **he who seeks finds;** and to him who knocks, the door will be opened" (Matthew 7:8 emphasis added). Our job as Hopekeepers is to pray that by His grace God will bring about this asking, seeking, and knocking in the hearts of our young people. I am keeping my hope alive that before long this young man will walk in total freedom from alcohol addiction. If you believe, not only for him but also for other young people in crisis, then join your faith with mine and say amen. "Amen!"

Seeing a Bigger Picture: Nations in the Making

There is a bigger picture that helps us to better understand the need for divine intervention. God is after the seed of nations that is in our young people.

The nations we are speaking of here are not political or geographical entities, but cultural people groups with distinguishing characteristics. Of these characteristics, the belief or faith system is the most critical, for it ultimately influences and shapes all other characteristics. God sees in our young people the potential for them to bring forth people groups or generations with belief systems that will either exalt or reject Him. Of course, His desire for them is that they will become generational links for the fulfillment of His eternal purpose.

In Genesis 25 when Rebekah inquired of the Lord about the struggle in her womb, He said to her, "Two nations are in your womb" (verse 23). In other words, the two sons in her womb would ultimately establish two different "cultures" based on two different belief or faith systems.

From the life stories of these two sons (Esau and Jacob) told in later chapters of the book of Genesis, we understand that through the younger son, Jacob, God continued the covenant of righteousness He had initiated with Abraham two generations earlier. That covenant was also a "culture" of righteousness built on faith in the true and living God.

God is concerned about the kind of nation or culture group that our young people will bring forth, and we must be too: There is a lot of talk these days about the subcultures that are influencing our young people, such as the drug, gun, and music subcultures. Many of our young people are in trouble or headed for trouble because they have been seduced by these evil subcultures. However, that is not their destiny.

God wants us to know that in spite of their present circumstances, our young people possess within them the potential to bring forth nations or cultures of righteousness. They will ultimately overcome the evil subcultures that have seduced them and move into their destiny to advance God's Kingdom. We cannot lose sight of the fact that every child that is conceived represents an emerging nation. Our children are the future of our nations in seed form.

An Intense Battle is Raging

Because of what our children and our young people represent, they are the objects of an extremely intense battle. On the one hand, God is seeking righteous seed to establish nations through which His dominion mandate given to humans can be carried out. On the other hand, however, Satan, the enemy of God and humanity, is seeking to kill, pollute, defile, and corrupt our offspring so that the reproach of sin might fall upon our nations. "Righteousness exalts a nation, but sin is a reproach to any people" (Proverbs 14:34 NKJV).

Against this background, we can sense the urgency for the restoration of our teens and young adults whose lives are in crisis. Many of them will become the next generation of parents, and we can not help wondering what kind of offspring they will bring forth.

According to the law of reproduction, our young people will bear fruit after their own kind. So as Hopekeepers we have to fight the good fight of faith for their lives to be turned around. By the grace and mercy of God, we will keep alive the hope that they will indeed fulfill their destiny as a righteous generation, and in turn produce the righteous offspring that God is seeking. Yes, there is hope! God's plan has always been for one generation to pass on a legacy of faith and righteousness to the next. (See Psalm 78:4-7.) God's plans and purposes will indeed prevail!

As we fight in this battle, our victory is dependent on this key principle: we must fight from a place of confident assurance of the victory Jesus has already won, confident of who we are in Christ and of the authority and power we have in Him.

Victory Has Already Been Won

Jesus has already conquered Satan and won the victory on behalf of our young people. He is the "Seed of the woman" that crushed the head of the serpent, as foretold by God in Genesis chapter three, verse fifteen. In Jesus' victory there is victory for every seed born of woman, including yours and mine.

Seeing our young people from this vantage point gives us great hope for their future because it means that the struggle is no longer just about them or about us. The battle is the Lord's! It is about the eternal plan that He has for the nations of the earth and His Kingdom. Our young people are the hope for the nations and the hope of God's Kingdom. Ultimately, this is the hope that we are keeping alive—God's hope—and His hope will not disappoint us.

Because of Jesus' victory, we as parents and other Hopekeepers living in relationship with Jesus and in covenant with God can confidently declare and enforce God's will in our young people's lives regardless of their present state. God intended them to be His righteous offspring, and that is what we hope for them to become. Standing in agreement with God's purposes puts us on His side of the battle—that means we are bound to win.

APPLICATION QUESTIONS
FOR
NO ORDINARY KIND OF INTERVENTION

1. Explain the importance of divine intervention in turning around our young people's crisis.
2. Why is divine intervention so often thought of as a last resort?
3. What advantage does the combination of natural and divine intervention offer? Think of a situation in which you have used or will use both types of intervention.
4. How does God's vested interest in our young people's crisis affect your perspective?
5. Are you prepared to enter into a covenant partnership with God for Him to intervene and restore our young people?

   A personal relationship with Jesus Christ is the first step in establishing that covenant. If you have never received Jesus as your personal Savior, I invite you to take that step now by praying these few words from your heart: *"Lord Jesus, I repent of my sins and ask you to be my Savior and Lord. Amen."* Also see Preparation Step #1 in Chapter 9.

Chapter Two

The Root of the Crisis

Homes and families everywhere are being devastated by the crises that are plaguing our teens and young adults. But the effect is even more far reaching. Schools, churches, the community, and the government are all grappling for solutions. Ultimately, the crises in the lives of our young people threaten to undermine the purposes of God on the earth.

When faced with any problem, we become more hopeful for a solution when we know at least two things: first, the cause of the problem and second, what it is going to take to fix it. In working toward any solution, we must first look at the symptoms that alert us to the existence of the problem.

Identifying the Symptoms

We are familiar with many of the symptoms of the crisis. They are what we referred to in the previous chapter as the face of the crisis: rebellion, excessive anger, attempted suicide, depression, sexual immorality, drug and alcohol addiction, violence and other criminal activities.

In one of his New Testament letters, the Apostle Paul writes about the dangers of the last days before Jesus returns to earth. The behaviors, attitudes, and lifestyles that he says will become evident in those days bear strong resemblance to what we are seeing in our generation of young people. The particular symptoms with which we are familiar may not be named specifically in the following passage, but I believe they fit somewhere in the description.

> But mark this: There will be terrible times in the last days. People will be lovers of themselves, lovers of money, boastful, proud, abusive, disobedient to their parents, ungrateful, unholy, without love, unforgiving, slanderous, without self-control, brutal, not lovers of the good, treacherous, rash, conceited, lovers of pleasure rather than lovers of God.... (2 Timothy 3:1-5)

Careful examination of the conditions reveals a primary symptom: the absence of a right relationship with God and others, especially parents. Our young people need the power and love of God operating through a personal relationship with Jesus Christ to help them overcome conditions such as these that are characteristic of the fallen human nature.

Many of our young people have become exposed to great danger because of estrangement from their parents. Disobedience and rebellion are the primary reasons for the breakdown of this vital relationship. Unfortunately, however, there are children and young people who have also been thrown into danger because of parental abandonment, neglect, and the abuse of parental authority. Families were created by God to be a safe haven, but many homes and families have been plagued with abuse, violence, and moral decadence. Instead of being places of refuge, they have become places of horror and major contributing factors to the crisis that many teens and young adults are facing.

Getting to the Root of the Problem

The symptoms of our young people's crisis are in many instances so blatant and extreme that if we are not careful we become consumed with them and never get to the root of the problem. The symptoms cannot be ignored, and many of them will require immediate, direct, practical action. But if we desire long-term permanent solutions, we need the wisdom of God to know what lies at the root and how to remedy it. As in health care, it may be necessary to first treat the pain or symptom before tackling the root of the problem.

This next passage of Scripture explicitly identifies some familiar symptoms and leads us directly to the root of the problem.

> For from within, out of men's hearts, come evil thoughts, sexual immorality, theft, murder, adultery, greed, malice, deceit, lewdness, envy, slander, arrogance and folly. All these evils come from inside.… (Mark 7:21-23)

There we have it. The heart, not the physical organ, but the spiritual heart lies at the root of the crisis.

Here is further evidence:

Keep your heart with all diligence;
For out of it springs the issues of life. (Proverbs 4:23 NKJV)

For as he thinks in his heart, so is he. (Proverbs 23:7 NKJV)

For out of the abundance of the heart the mouth speaks. A good man out of the good treasure of his heart brings forth good things, and an evil man out of the evil treasure brings forth evil things. (Matthew 12:34b-35 NKJV)

What are these passages of Scripture telling us? They are revealing truths that apply to all humanity. But from them we can gain much insight into our young people's fundamental issues and needs.

1. The heart (the spiritual heart) is the source or foundation upon which an individual's life is built.

2. As with a house that over time starts developing structural problems because of its poor foundation, the fruit or manifestation of an individual's life (behaviors, attitudes and actions) ultimately reflects the individual's spiritual heart condition.

We are going to be examining some of the many factors that work upon a person's heart to make it what it is, but first let's define the spiritual heart and do a further diagnosis of the root problem.

The Spiritual Heart Defined

By the spiritual heart I am referring to the core or center of a person's being, where both the conscious and unconscious memories of everything that person has ever experienced are stored. Unfortunately for some of our young people, it is the stored memories of unhealed hurts and unresolved issues that are now being manifested as destructive lifestyles.

- The heart is the place from which our convictions about life, our values, attitudes, decisions, words, behavior, and character originate.
- The heart is not the same as the spirit or the soul of man, but it encompasses dimensions of both. We often use the words spirit and heart interchangeably, but the Scriptures differentiate them by using different Hebrew and Greek words.
- It may be thought of as the subconscious mind since it stores unconscious memories.
- It is the part of our being in which we believe, understand, and appropriate spiritual truths. "For with the heart one believes to righteousness" (Romans 10:10a NKJV).

The Diagnosis: A Heart Problem and a Crisis of Identity

In addition to learning from the Scriptures that the outward expressions of our lives originate in the heart, we also learn that what is in our hearts defines who we are. That is what Proverbs 23:7 means. "For as he thinks in his heart, so is he." In other words, what is in our hearts, or the condition of our hearts, shapes our sense of identity.

When a strong foundation is not laid in the heart during our early years to orient us or incline our hearts toward God, to sustain a relationship with Jesus Christ, to know who we are as God's offspring, and to know the purpose for which He made us, our later years will in all likelihood be fraught with searching, experimentation, vulnerability to Satan's deception, and wrong choices. The crisis in many of our young people's lives stems from this crisis of identity.

As we observe the process of human development, we recognize that we are most vulnerable to this crisis at the transitional stages of life. The transitions from childhood to adolescence and from adolescence to adulthood are particularly precarious. They are marked by an inherent need for independence from parental influence. This need expresses itself in a quest to discover one's own sense of personhood and to establish one's own system of beliefs and values.

These are not bad things in and of themselves. They are a natural part of the maturation process. The problem arises if the foundation of our early years is not strong enough to withstand the transition. Only a heart anchored in the truth of God's Word and relationship with Jesus Christ can safeguard against the rebellion and other potential dangers that these transitional stages of life present.

From what we have discovered in the Scriptures, we may draw these conclusions about the root of our young people's crisis.

- The outward conditions being manifested in their lives are symptoms, or the fruit, of a crisis of identity that originated in the heart which is shaped by factors such as childhood experiences and the lack of a right relationship with God and parents.
- Since their hearts' condition is at the root of the crisis, any solution that seeks to produce long-term, lasting change must target the heart.

- To be successful, efforts to change their attitudes, moral behavior, choices, and actions must be coupled with strategies that produce a change of heart.
- A change of heart is possible only by the power of Jesus Christ as His Spirit indwells them and gives them new hearts.

Millions of dollars are now being spent on government-sponsored and private programs to combat the outbreak of gangs, drugs, and gun violence in many communities. While these agencies are to be commended for their efforts, there is a need to be aware that unless they deepen their focus to the heart, the improvements they achieve will only be short-lived.

This book is a step in that direction. The primary goal of this book is to engage parents and others who may not otherwise be involved, to become part of the solution through the practice of strategies that will bring about divine intervention. The involvement of parents is critical, because from God's perspective they have the greatest spiritual authority to influence the hearts of their sons and daughters, regardless of their age and circumstances.

Understanding How the Heart Is Shaped

The dangerous thing about the heart is that we never truly know the full potential of evil that lurks within it. Because we do not know all that is in our hearts, we can be easily deceived by them. The heart is deceitful above all things, and desperately wicked: who can know it? (Jeremiah 17:9 KJV). The New International Version translation says it is "beyond cure."

In exploring the root of the crisis that is plaguing our young people, it helps to understand how the heart got to be the way it is. Often the tendency is to think that it is entirely our young people's fault that they ended up where they are. It is true that they are ultimately responsible for their own choices. But some of what I have discovered may come as a big surprise: It is not all their fault, and it is not all the devil's fault either.

Most qualities of the heart are shaped in the early years of life and are directly influenced by generational legacies. Many of us as parents have been ignorant of these principles, so we did not do anything to stop the perpetuation of negative tendencies. But let me hasten to say that this is by no means a statement of parental blame or guilt.

So just what factors have influenced the hearts of our young people?

First, there is the sin nature that they, like all human beings, have inherited from Adam, the first man. We are all born with the potential for evil that in time will be activated and released in one way or another if it is not harnessed at an early age. According to Genesis 8:21, "every inclination of his [the] heart is evil from childhood."

Second, there is the generational legacy they inherited. As part of that legacy, they inherited certain spiritual heart dispositions from their parents and ancestors; these are coded into their DNA just as physical characteristics are.

The third factor is our own parental shortcomings. (Ouch! Remember that this is not about blame or guilt. Our objective is to get to the root of a serious problem and find appropriate solutions.) In ignorance many of us used disciplinary methods that aimed solely at behavior modification without getting at the heart condition that produced the behavior, and without turning the orientation of the heart toward godly character. We may have spoken negative words in frustration and anger, or poorly represented the shepherd's heart of God our heavenly Father. We may also have practiced religious routines instead of modeling a personal intimate relationship with the Lord. These are some of the areas in which we may have fallen short of God's intent.

The fourth factor is their personal response to unfavorable circumstances and their individual life experiences. These responses which started from the moment they were conceived in the womb, are a major factor in shaping the attitudes, character and choices that our young people are now manifesting.

The final factor is the environment in which they live. It acts as a catalyst to activate the potential of their hearts, whether for good or evil. Here I am referring to the social culture in general, as well as the environment of home, school and peers.

What About the Good We Did?

Some parents are still asking the questions that I used to ask: "What happened? What went wrong?" We think of the earlier years when our children were young. We spent time teaching them how to pray; we taught them Bible verses and read Bible stories to them. We took them to church with us (most of us did not just send them), and we do not know what happened to those good influences.

Well, from my own parenting experiences and from what others have shared with me, I have now come to understand a few things:

- We by-passed the heart when it should have been the focus and target of their training and nurturing.
- We may have been fooled by their apparent innocence, unaware of the evil potential within the heart that needed to be dealt with.
- We may have mistakenly thought that we needed to wait until they were intellectually responsive to introduce the Word of God to them, and in doing so we missed the most critical time for programming or reconstituting their hearts.
- We may not have sustained what we started. It is possible that lapses in our own relationship with the Lord and an inconsistent Christian lifestyle could have opened the door and created opportunities for the enemy.
- Many of us also did not realize that we needed to cut ourselves off in the spirit realm from unrighteous generational legacies. It is only in recent years that we have started to hear much teaching on this matter.

So, unintentionally and by default, we fostered an environment that nurtured rather than destroyed the propensity and potential for evil that lurked in our children's hearts.

All Is Still Not Lost

How I love the Lord, for He never condemns us for our ignorance and mistakes! He has graciously encouraged me with much insight, and I want to pass on the same encouragement to you.

It is never too late to get back on track and turn things around. All is not lost!

We may have been late in starting to sow seeds of righteousness into the hearts of our children, but whatever seeds we have sowed have not all died. Some have been snatched away or choked out, but some have remained. They may be covered over by many negative things, but there is still life in them.

God has shown me a picture of young plants bursting out of rocks and concrete. The root of righteousness is not fully cut off. It is still connected to the life source. There is a time for every activity under heaven, and at the right season of our young people's lives, pressure from the life force within the incorruptible seed of righteousness that was planted in them will break through every barrier. Let's start praying for the spring rains to fall on these dormant seeds.

Our young people in whom God's Word was planted may have strayed away in the same way that the children of Israel did. But God spoke concerning their restoration, and His Word concerning them is also true for our young people. "But as a terebinth or oak tree leaves a stump when it is cut down, so Israel's stump will be a holy seed" (Isaiah 6:13 NLT).

Here is another promise:

For there is hope for a tree,
If it is cut down, that it will sprout again,
And that its tender shoots will not cease.
Though its root may grow old in the earth,
And its stump may die in the ground,
Yet at the scent of water it will bud
And bring forth branches like a plant. (Job 14:7-9 NKJV)

Did you catch the hope in that Word? I say, "Amen, Lord! So be it!" Now, our part is to let our prayers, decrees, declarations and proclamations be the "scent of water" going to the root of our young people's lives.

As you read what we had to say about early seeds of righteousness, you may be a parent who is thinking, *What if I did not sow any seeds of righteousness?* All is still not lost! Jesus is the true Seed, and it is not too late for you to fill your heart with the Word of God and start sending it to the heart of your son or daughter. In time, that Word will produce a miraculous harvest that I like to think of as a miraculous explosion of the Jesus seed.

What do I mean? Jesus is the living Word, the living Seed, and Life itself. By the grace of God, when He comes into a heart, He is able to miraculously explode and infuse His Life into that heart. Jesus is able to make up for lost time, accelerate, and transform a life by turning tragedies into triumphs and messes into messages.

Jesus is able to make up for lost time, accelerate, and transform a life by turning tragedies into triumphs and messes into messages.

God is doing something in the spiritual realm that we will never see if we keep looking at things in the natural. One day the Holy Spirit said to me, "Take your eyes off your children. What you are going through is not just about them, and it is not just about you either. I am preparing some things for the generations to come." How encouraged I was to hear those words!

I believe with all my heart that God is going to use Satan's own weapons against him. God is preparing for Himself a new breed of deliverers for the next generation.

We often think that it is primarily those who have always walked in God's ways who are used mightily by God. But that is not it at all. God uses anyone and anything. We need to see that the areas of struggle and crisis that our young people are dealing with are the very areas in which they will become mighty deliverers for God.

Who can be a better witness of God's power to deliver from drugs, alcohol, prostitution, violence and abuse than someone who has personally been delivered from these by the mighty hand of God? Their testimony will be exceptionally powerful. Through their personal knowledge and first-hand experience of God's love and mercy, they will be able to bear witness passionately and effectively to others about who God really is, and the power of Jesus' redemption.

My friend, this thing is bigger than any one of us. All we have to do is cooperate with God and watch Him go to work. Do what He requires of you and keep your hope alive.

Evil Increases with Each Generation

I have spoken with parents and others who have great difficulty appreciating the dangers that this generation of teens and young adults faces as they pass into adulthood. They do not understand it because they survived their transitional stages just fine. What many fail to understand, however, is that evil increases in each age.

Knowing his time is coming to an end, Satan is intensifying his demand on the potential of the sin nature that is in us. He is particularly targeting the younger generation, for they are the key to our nation's future.

Many of us may think that some of the things we did in our younger days were pretty bad. But I believe we have not seen anything yet. If we do not fight for our young people to be rescued from the power of Satan, we who are parents will wonder how under God's heaven we could have birthed such monsters, or how they could have come from our family line.

A Vision of Hope

As much as evil has been increasing with each generation, so has God's holy anger against Satan. Satan has been having a field day, and God is not pleased. In fact, God has been greatly concerned about the conditions in which many of our young people have found themselves. He has roused Himself in holy anger and is ready to contend for their restoration.

At a prayer meeting one night, one of my Hopekeeper partners received a powerful vision of hope. She saw Jesus bent in intercession, pained and declaring: "Forbid them not! Forbid them not!" He then took the children that were being forbidden, both the young and the older ones, into His arms and invoked a blessing upon them. (See Mark 10:13-16 and Luke 18:16.)

The rest of what she saw in the vision was quite vivid. In Jesus' pained intercession and strong declaration, everything that had hindered the children from coming to Him was being exposed and destroyed. As Jesus cried out, "Forbid them not," it was as if heaven's excavation crew was digging up things that were buried, things underground that were forbidding or hindering the children from coming to Jesus. Things on earth that had kept them in bondage had to obey the shouted command of Jesus. Things in the heavenlies—assignments, assaults, corrupt plans, evil legislation, and judgments—that were being prepared for earth against them, had to be aborted. Jesus was crying out for the children. His intercession for them was so intense that His heart was bleeding.

She explained that in the prayer meeting they also started to contend for the children, speaking to the four corners of the earth to release them. The vision ended with Jesus sitting on a rock, His hands dripping with honey, and the children coming to Him and licking His hands.

Her revelation about this last part of the vision fills us with hope for the restoration of our young people. Jesus was giving them a real taste of Himself. He was redeeming their taste from the perversion and defilement and corruption. Their sense of taste was being made new. They started desiring spiritual things. They desired Him as He really is. They were so satisfied, so fulfilled.

Doesn't that make you want to shout? Go ahead. Hallelujah! Thank you, Jesus!

God is ready to deliver our young people as He delivered the children of Israel that were enslaved in Egypt. With our cooperation God's miraculous power will manifest for them as it did for the children of Israel. As we read in the biblical account of their exodus from Egypt, Moses had to cooperate with God in bringing about their deliverance, and so must we.

We are God's present-day Moses cooperating with Him for the deliverance of a generation of young people. By God's grace we will cooperate. We are going to fight on their behalf. And we will not give up or give in either. As long as there is breath in our bodies we will keep our hope alive. And even after we have finished our work here on the earth, we trust God that our seeds of hope will continue to produce a harvest in future generations so that our families and nations will be established in righteousness.

A New Heart

The successful deliverance and restoration of our young people will come as we target their hearts. We have now established that what lies at the root of their crisis is a heart that has been defiled. They are suffering from spiritual heart disease, and they need a change of heart— a new heart.

The successful deliverance and restoration of our young people will come as we target their hearts.

We cannot expect our young people to do for themselves what we as older adults can not even do for ourselves. We know how hard it is to change the things about ourselves that need to be changed. Many of us have been grappling with certain things for years. The truth is that real change is the work of grace, not possible to be achieved by our own efforts.

And what is grace? Grace is much more than unmerited favor. You will see what I mean by these two definitions:

> Grace is God's ability working in man, making him able to do what he cannot do in his own ability. [1]

> It is God's divine influence upon your heart, and the reflection of that influence in your life. [2]

In 2 Corinthians 6:1 where the Apostle Paul urges us not to receive the grace of God in vain, the Amplified Bible elaborates on grace as, "that merciful kindness by which God exerts His holy influence on souls and turns them to Christ, keeping and strengthening them...."

Grace is the divine influence by which God's saving, restorative, keeping, and strengthening power is imparted to humanity. This divine influence is released by, and works through faith, which is exactly what the strategies in this book are aiming to bring about.

> For it is by grace you have been saved, through faith. (Ephesians 2:8a)

> Let us then approach the throne of grace with confidence, so that we may receive mercy and **find grace** to help us in our time of need. (Hebrews 4:16 emphasis added)

> See to it that no one misses the grace of God. (Hebrews 12:15a)

Heart Surgery

I was preparing to speak to a group of youths, parents, and mentors on this subject when the Holy Spirit gave me a somewhat comical but strong word. "They need heart surgery, but it will not be 'heart bypass surgery.' Their hearts have been 'bypassed' enough. Now they have to be turned for me to give them a new heart. They need a heart transplant."

> I will sprinkle clean water on you, and you will be clean; I will cleanse you from all your impurities and from all your idols. I will give you a new heart and put a new spirit in you; I will remove from you your heart of stone and give you a heart of flesh. And I will put my Spirit in you and move you to follow my decrees and be careful to keep my laws. (Ezekiel 36:25-27)

> "This is the covenant I will make with [them]!
>   after that time," declares the LORD.
>   "I will put my law in their minds
>   and write it on their hearts.

> I will be their God,
> and they will be my people.
> No longer will a man teach his neighbor,
> or a man his brother, saying, 'Know the LORD,'
> because they will all know me,
> from the least of them to the greatest,"
> declares the LORD.
> "For I will forgive their wickedness
> and will remember their sins no more." (Jeremiah 31:33-34)

In the natural, as you know, a heart transplant is a highly complicated surgical procedure. It is the same way in the spiritual. But God is well able and never fails. Just as there is preparation work for a physical heart transplant, there is also spiritual preparation work. The prayers, declarations, decrees and words of hope that you will find in Part II of this book are for that very purpose. They are expressions of the Word of God, which releases God's power and grace to turn the hearts of our young people to Jesus for Him to change their lives.

As we are faithful in doing our part, we will see the miracles of God take place before our very eyes. Jesus, the Master Surgeon, will work on the hearts of our young people at times and in ways that we least expect. Let's be faithful, keep our hope alive and expect the miraculous.

APPLICATION POINTS
FOR
THE ROOT OF THE CRISIS

1. Explain the relationship between the spiritual heart and symptoms of crisis as manifested in our young people's behavior, attitudes and actions.
2. How has the awareness of this relationship between the heart and our life expressions helped you to better understand the dynamics of change in yourself and others?
3. Ask the Holy Spirit to reveal to you the hidden secrets of the heart of the teen or young adult with whom you are directly or indirectly involved.
4. What specific revelation in this chapter gives you hope that all is not lost?

For Hopekeeper Parents

5. Can you identify any parental shortcomings that might have contributed to your son's or daughter's heart condition? If you can not, ask the Holy Spirit to reveal to you anything you need to know. Remember that God is not condemning you.

Quick Prayer Points

- Lord, forgive me (or _____'s parents) for any way in which I/they may have contributed negatively to the shaping of _____'s heart.
- In the name of Jesus, I ask Father that you would pour out your grace upon _____ and give him/her a new heart.

Chapter Three

Encouragement for Parents and Other Hopekeepers

O n this journey of hope for the restoration of our teens and young people, there is no Scripture that encourages me like this one:

This is what the LORD says:
> "Restrain your voice from weeping
> and your eyes from tears,
> for your work will be rewarded,"
> declares the LORD.
> "They will return from the land of the enemy.
> So there is hope for your future,"
> declares the LORD.
> "Your children will return to their own land." (Jeremiah 31:16-17)

God's Promise of Hope

Deep in my heart and the heart of all well-meaning parents is the desire that our offspring will accomplish more and go farther than we have. We love our children and want only what is best for them We want to see God's plans for their lives fulfilled. So it is natural for us to hurt and fall into despair when the crises in their lives threaten our hope for their future.

I believe it also breaks the heart of other Hopekeepers to see the precious potential of the young people around them being wasted.

But God promises us hope. Our young people will return from the land of the enemy. They will return to their own land. The promise spoken by God through the prophet Jeremiah was initially given by God to the Israelites concerning the return of the Babylonian exiles. However, we can claim that same promise for the spiritual return of our young people from every kind of crisis into which they have fallen.

That is right—our offspring and other young people will return from the land of waywardness, rebellion, anger, abuse, addictions, violence, and even imprisonment into which the enemy has seduced them. They will return from the land of the enemy to the land of a fruitful relationship with God, to the land of purpose and destiny that God has prepared for them. They will return from the abandonment of their faith to put their trust once more in the saving power of Jesus Christ.

If you are reading this and wondering how you are going to remain hopeful when the situation is so dismal, start saying what God's Word says:

I can do all things through Christ who strengthens me. (Philippians 4:13 NKJV)

With man this is impossible, but not with God; all things are possible with God. (Mark 10:27)

The Lord Almighty, Most High God, our Creator and heavenly Father, wants to see the lives of our young people turned around more than we do. They are His offspring, and His hope for the future of humanity is wrapped up in them.

Our sons and daughters belonged to God before He gave them to us. He knew them and loved them even before we did. I like the way that The Message Bible paraphrases John 17:6, "They were yours in the first place; then you gave them to me." That is what Jesus said concerning His disciples, but it is also true of our sons and daughters and the other young people that God has brought into our lives.

God chose them before He even laid the foundation of the world. He sent them to the earth for a purpose and has made provision for each one to fulfill his or her unique purpose. (See Ephesians 1:4 and 2:10.) Many of our young people have gone off course, but it is not too late. Neither are they too far gone to get back on track.

You Have What It Takes

Perhaps you have heard the expression that God provides for what He demands. Well, it applies to us as God's Hopekeepers for young people that are in crisis. God would not have given you the responsibility for your son or daughter or a desire to help other young people if He had not also given you what it takes, with His help, to take a stand and fight for their destiny. He has equipped you for this and is counting on you to be faithful.

God is a mighty deliverer, and with our cooperation He will turn things around.

God is a mighty deliverer, and with our cooperation He will turn things around. Our cooperation begins with keeping hope alive—trusting in God and having a positive attitude about the present and future of our young people.

A Personal Revelation

Let me share a personal experience with you. There was a time when I became so overwhelmed with concerns for my grown children that, without realizing it, my hope started slipping. One morning in prayer, the Lord showed me that I had been trusting more in the enemy's power to seduce and ensnare them than in His power to set them free. Of course, He was right; so I repented right away.

That day the Lord revealed something very encouraging that I believe will also encourage you. He said: "I train my servants in the place and in the thing I designed them to have the most influence. But I need human agents to carry them through on faith, prayers, and their proclamation of my Word. As a parent you are my principal agent for restoring your offspring that are in crisis."

He then went on to explain that He is the God who knows and sees all things. He does not control the choices our young people are making, and their crisis is not His plan for their lives. However, by His sovereign power, He does control the outcome of all things. He is very economical and will allow no trial, test or crisis to be wasted.

From what may be considered the broken fragments of our young people's lives, Jesus will make something beautiful and will Himself fulfill the words He spoke on the occasion of the feeding of the five thousand. "Gather the pieces that are left over. Let nothing be wasted" (John 6:12). Every single crisis will contribute to the fulfillment of God's divine purpose for our young people's lives if we will exercise faith on their behalf and cooperate with God while they are going through these phases of life.

As the Lord revealed these things to me, I started to see our young people's crisis from another perspective. I started seeing them as potential servants of God. I started to see that although their lives did not currently bring honor to God, by His power and by His grace, He is able to use the things they are going through as preparation for ministering to those whom they will serve in their generation.

I realized that their exposure to the subcultures of their generation would enable them to identify with and later influence many for God's Kingdom. But this exposure is meant to be temporary, the Lord revealed, and we as Hopekeepers have the responsibility to ensure that it does not become permanent by watching over their souls. Our young people do not really know what is going on. The devil does not quite understand it either. Much of it is even outside of his control. But it is all in God's sovereign control, and He wants us to know this.

God Requires Our Faithfulness

As we remain faithful in prayer for God's grace to abound toward our young people and bring about restoration in their lives, He will indeed cause all things to work together for their good. He will take that which the enemy meant for evil and turn it to good. The Holy Spirit is our Helper, and He will teach us how to speak words of faith, love and hope to bring about the fulfillment of every one of God's good plans for them.

God knows that doing this alone is difficult, especially when we are not sure what to do. He knows all about our challenges, and that is why He connects us with others in similar circumstances. I thank God for the opportunity to bring you this message of hope.

I believe God has connected us through this resource because He wants you to rise up as one of His faithful Hopekeepers. I do not know where your hope is at this time, and it really does not matter. Have you lost hope? It is time to regain it. And if your hope has been dashed to the ground, it is time to pick it up. If you are just about to slide into hopelessness, stop! Hold on, and start recovering what you have allowed to slip. However, if by the grace of God you have been keeping your hope alive, I encourage you to keep on fighting the good fight of faith, for in due season you shall reap if you faint not.

God has connected us through this resource because He wants you to rise up as one of His faithful Hopekeepers.

For all of us, the prayer of my heart is that we will remain faithful, abound in hope and never let go. As of this day, we will be those who stand firm, keeping hope alive for the restoration of our young people, regardless of their circumstances.

You can not wait for the circumstances to change before you start having hope. In fact, it is unlikely that it will change without hope. So, hope now! Proverbs 13:12 says, "Hope deferred makes the heart sick, but a longing fulfilled is a tree of life." Receive the Spirit of hope. Sow hope now, and you shall reap a harvest of fulfillment.

By faith in the authority of Jesus' name, I release the power of Romans 15:13 into you as a Hopekeeper: "Now may the God of hope fill you with all joy and peace in believing, so that you will abound in hope by the power of the Holy Spirit" (NAS).

Did you notice how that verse started? It started with "Now." Be filled with hope now! Not later, not tomorrow, not next week, not when the situation improves. Be filled with hope now! May the God of hope fill—yes—fill you with all joy and peace in believing. ALL! That is right, *all* joy and peace. A full measure of hope, joy and peace is yours through believing. So that you may abound—yes, abound—overflow—with hope. The Amplified translation says, "that...you may abound and be overflowing (bubbling over) with hope." Hallelujah!

We will abound and overflow in hope which will come about not in our own strength but by the power of the Holy Spirit. By ourselves we can do nothing. As the Scriptures tell us, we accomplish nothing by our own natural might or power but only by the might and power of the Holy Spirit. (See Zechariah 4:6.)

Your Role as God's Hopekeeper

As you read farther along, it will become much clearer to you what it means to be God's Hopekeeper. For now, let me share with you some preliminary thoughts on what your role as one of God's Hopekeepers accomplishes for our young people in crisis.

- You make up the hedge and stand in the gap on their behalf so they are not destroyed. (See Ezekiel 22:30.)
- You repair and restore the broken down, waste places in their lives. (See Isaiah 61:4.)
- You are God's present-day Moses who will help to deliver them out of bondage. (See Exodus chapter 3.)
- You are their Nehemiah committed to the rebuilding of the spiritual walls of protection around their lives so they are not disgraced. (See Nehemiah chapters 1-4.)
- You are God's warriors fighting as in the days of Nehemiah, and standing against the forces of darkness that are seeking to seduce, oppress, and destroy our generation of young people. (See Nehemiah 4:14, Ephesians 6:10-12.)

- You are functioning as God's royal priesthood—as a priest lifting them up to God, and as a king establishing heaven's will and rule in their lives. (See 1 Peter 2:9.)
- You are engaged in a ministry of reconciliation for the turning of the hearts of a generation of young people back to God; for fathers to be turned to children and children to fathers. (See Malachi 4:6, 2 Corinthians 5:18.)
- You are the voice of one crying in the wilderness, preparing the way for God's intervention. (See Isaiah 40:3-5, John 1:23.)
- You are giving God the legal access He needs to intervene in their lives. (See Matthew 16:19-20; 18:18-20.)

Spiritual Access Codes

Your prayers, your declarations and decrees, your agreement with the Word of God, and your praise are like spiritual access codes that open the door for God to intervene in the lives of young people.

Do you see why the Bible puts so much emphasis on making our requests known to God? I used to think that asking was for our sake only. But it is also for God's sake. God knows every need and desire we have, and wants to fulfill them more than we can imagine. However, He does require that we ask of Him. (See Matthew 7:7-11, 21:22; John 14:13-14; James 4:2; Philippians 4:6.)

There is a similar emphasis in the Scriptures on speaking forth decrees, proclamations and commands. We see Jesus doing this as He rebuked evil spirits, ordered a storm to cease and declared that a fig tree would never again bear fruit. He also taught that we can do the same things that He did. We can have what we say as long as there is no doubt in our hearts and we expect what we say to come to pass. We have the authority and power from Jesus to speak forth God's will for it to be established on the earth. (See Job 22:28 KJV; Mark 9:25; Mark 11:12-14, 20-25.)

I heard an expression some time ago that really nails down this principle concerning God's operation in the earth: *If we don't, God won't.* That is just the way God designed the earth to operate, so let us cooperate with Him and see our young people's lives restored.

Guard Against Discouragement

Be aware that as you seek to cooperate with God as a Hopekeeper for our young people, Satan will try to use the weapon of discouragement against you. He will try to kill your hope. But as the Psalmist encouraged Israel in the Songs of Ascent, so I encourage you.

> Put your hope in the LORD,
> for with the LORD is unfailing love
> and with him is full redemption.
> He himself will redeem [your offspring]
> from all their sins. (Psalm 130:7-8)

> Be strong and take heart,
> all you who hope in the LORD. (Psalm 31:24)

> Put your hope in the LORD
> both now and forevermore. (Psalm 131:3)

Like King David, when discouragement comes, encourage yourself in the Lord with His Word. Feed and nourish your hope with God's Word. Speak words of life to your own soul.

> Why are you downcast, O my soul?
> Why so disturbed within me?
> Put your hope in God,
> for I will yet praise him,
> my Savior and my God. (Psalm 42:5)

> I wait for the LORD, my soul waits,
> and in his word I put my hope.

My soul waits for the Lord
> more than watchmen wait for the morning,
> more than watchmen wait for the morning. (Psalm 130:5-6)

Anchor yourself in the promise God makes to you in His Word:

I am the LORD; those who hope in me will not be disappointed. (Isaiah 49:23b)

No one whose hope is in [me] will ever be put to shame. (Psalm 25:3a)

And respond with this commitment of faith:

> But, as for me, I will always have hope;
> > I will praise you more and more. (Psalm 71:14)

Praise the Lord!

APPLICATION POINTS
FOR
ENCOURAGEMENT FOR PARENTS AND OTHER HOPEKEEPERS

1. Ask the Lord to help you develop a picture, image, and vision of what your restored teen or young adult will be like.
2. Why is it so easy to fall into the trap of trusting more in the enemy's power to seduce and ensnare our young people than in God's power to set them free?
3. What steps will you take to avoid this temptation?
4. What is the relationship between Romans 8:28 and the hope you have for the restoration of your teen or young adult?
5. Personalize and memorize Romans 15:13 to keep your hope alive.
6. Review the nine dimensions of your role as a Hopekeeper, and read the Scriptures related with each one.
7. Which of the nine dimensions of your role as a Hopekeeper appeal to you the most? Why?

Chapter Four

The Anchor of Our Hope

H ave you ever noticed that hope, like love, makes all the difference in a person's life and in the lives of those around them?

If you want to know just how powerful hope is, imagine for a moment, if you can, what it must be like for individuals who commit suicide. They actually got swallowed up by despair and despondency; they lost all hope then hit rock bottom. You will agree that we definitely need hope in order to live from day to day, especially when things are at their worst.

What Exactly is Hope?

Hope is a commonly used word that means different things to different people. But I want to be sure that we have the same understanding of what it means. After all, if we are going to be keeping our hope alive, it is important that we agree on what it is that we are really talking about.

Let's explore some definitions.

The dictionary defines hope as "an expectation that what one desires will happen."

This next definition gives us a biblical point of view: "Hope means desire married to expectation. It is the happy anticipation of good…not only *the desire for,* but the *expectation of* God's blessings, God's provision, God's power and the fulfillment of His promise."[1]

Elaborating on the word *hope,* the Amplified Bible translates it as "[the habit] of joyful and confident expectation of eternal salvation." (See Romans 5:4; 1 Corinthians 13:13.)

From these definitions, we may compile the following thoughts for our purposes:

- Hope is much more than wishful thinking, optimism, or positive thinking.
- Hope is a settled, God-based confidence and assurance.
- Hope is the earnest expectation of something desired.
- Hope comes with supernatural and intense expectancy that what we are expecting to happen will happen to bring about the improvement of a condition in spite of natural circumstances.

Although the dictionary does not bring this out, our day-to-day use of the word carries with it a negative sense of doubt and disappointment. For example, when someone says they hope something will happen, they are really expressing a wish and implying at the same time that it may not come true. Hedged in there somewhere is the possibility of disappointment.

In the biblical sense, however, hope is entirely positive. As the Apostle Paul wrote in one of his epistles, "hope does not disappoint us" (Romans 5:5). This is the kind of hope that we are keeping alive for our young people. The question is where and how do we get it?

God is the unlimited, unfailing source of true hope.

The Scriptures refer to God as the "God of hope," and "our hope" (Romans 15:13; 1 Timothy 1:1). We can, therefore, conclude that God is the unlimited, unfailing source of true hope, and through His unchangeable Word, He transmits and transfers that hope to us.

Possessing this God-begotten kind of hope takes time. It is a process that requires us to receive and conceive God's Word in our hearts by faith, meditate on it, and speak it forth. And it is by continually believing and trusting in His Word that we nourish, feed, and keep our hope alive.

Partners of Hope

Hope is a powerful force, but it does not work by itself. First Corinthians 13:13 describes the other forces that partner with hope. "And now these three remain: faith, hope and love. But the greatest of these is love."

These forces work together like a three-fold cord that is not easily broken. Let's look at how they operate.

- Love is the greatest of all three, for it is the source, basis, and means by which faith and hope express themselves. (See Galatians 5:6b KJV.)
- Hope sets the goal by creating an image of a desired future, and gives direction to faith. Hope is like the blueprint from which faith works. (See Hebrews 11:1 KJV.)
- Faith is the substance or material that produces the end result of hope. (See Hebrews 11:1 KJV.)

In summary, hope is essential for victory, for where there is no hope, there will be no pathway to take us there. Hope is powerful, but it cannot accomplish its goal on its own. In order to do its work, hope must be accompanied by faith which works through love.

It is love that motivates us to fight for our young people's restoration and to keep our hope and faith alive. It is love that enables us to defy their present reality and dare to believe that the future God intended for them is attainable.

Love, hope and faith are not passive forces by any means. They must be put to work through words and actions, and that is why in Part II we have compiled many faith-filled words of hope for you to speak in love.

The Only Sure Anchor for Hope

Hope works in partnership with love and faith, and, as we will now see, it also needs the right anchor to work effectively. People have anchored their hope on many things. But as a Hopekeeper, you want to make sure that your hope is anchored in something secure—something that will not change, fail, or slip when storms arise.

The only sure anchor for our hope is the God of hope Himself, His Word, and everything He provides through Jesus Christ. He is the all-powerful God who is able to do whatever He promises. Every word He speaks and every promise He makes are backed by His unfailing power.

Here are some anchors for you to hook into right now.

As for God, his way is perfect;
    the word of the LORD is flawless.
He is a shield
    for all who take refuge in him. (Psalm 18:30)

You are my refuge and my shield;
    I have put my hope in your word. (Psalm 119:114)

I wait for the LORD, my soul waits,
    and in his word I put my hope. (Psalm 130:5)

The Old Testament provides us with a powerful illustration of hope in the lives of Abraham and Sarah. Both of them were almost a hundred years old when God told them they would have a child. In the natural there was no hope, no possibility, of this happening, but God said that they would.

You will always find hope in God's word regardless of how dismal a situation may appear.

Well, what did Abraham do? The Bible says that "against hope he believed in hope." In other words, although there was no hope in the natural, Abraham anchored himself in supernatural hope. He agreed with God and believed in God's faithfulness and power to fulfill what He had promised. He believed in the God who calls things visible only in the spirit realm as though they were already visible in the natural. (See Romans 4:17-18; Hebrews 11:8-19.)

You can count on this, my fellow Hopekeeper. You will always find hope in God's Word regardless of how dismal a situation may appear. You can always speak God's Word about a situation that appears hopeless, and actually inject hope back into it. You can also wield God's Word as His Spirit sword to cut off discouragement and everything that would try to kill your hope. You will notice that the word sword is "word" with an "s" in front. To me that is very significant. On the one hand, God's Word is your anchor and, on the other, it is your sword.

How long should you keep your hope alive? To the end—until you see the manifestation of what you are hoping for.

> Wherefore gird up the loins of your mind, be sober, and **hope to the end** for the grace that is to be brought unto you at the revelation of Jesus Christ. (1 Peter 1:13 KJV emphasis added)

The revelation of Jesus Christ does not only mean His return or second coming. We can also take it to mean Jesus Christ showing up in the life and circumstances of our young people when we summon or invite Him to get involved in their crises.

As a Hopekeeper, you need to realize that it will take time for the Word of God to be conceived in your heart and produce the faith that is necessary to see your hope fulfilled.

God is a God of miracles, but miracles are not always sudden or instantaneous. We read about many instances where healing and deliverance occurred suddenly in the Bible. However, even in those cases there was a process of faith leading up to the sudden manifestations.

There is amazing strength and power in God's Word. God's Word formed in our hearts and spoken consistently out of our mouths is guaranteed to break through any crisis. That is another anchor of hope right there. Let's thank God for it.

Thank you for the strength and power of your Word, Lord. Let it be formed in our hearts and in our mouths and come forth like a mighty force bringing deliverance to our sons and daughters. In Jesus' name. Amen.

Reasons for Our Hope Anchor

Here now is a quick list of reasons why God and His Word are such strong anchors for our hope.

1. God has all power to fulfill His Word.
2. God never fails and He never changes.
3. God is the God of hope.
4. God is faithful to all His promises.
5. Every Word of God will be fulfilled in its proper or appointed time, because He watches over His Word to perform it.
6. God's credibility is at stake in His Word.
7. God's Word is guaranteed to do the work it is sent to do, and will never return to Him empty, void or unproductive.
8. God's Word is the incorruptible, indestructible and eternal seed to be planted in the heart to save the soul and produce a harvest of righteousness.
9. God's Word is spirit, life, and truth.
10. God's Word activates the highest spiritual law, which is the law of the Spirit of life in Christ Jesus that sets us free from the law of sin and death.
11. God's Word is creative substance. It is the power and energy by which God created the heavens and the earth.
12. God's Word is divine currency. In the economy of God's Kingdom, we obtain His desired reality for our lives by speaking forth His Word in faith.
13. God's Word is the sword that your spirit wields. It is sharp, active, quick, and powerful. It is a two-edged sword for defense and offense.
14. God's Word is multi-functional. It has the ability to pierce, divide, discern, burn, break, wash and cleanse. It is fire that

burns, a hammer that shatters, a sword that pierces, the seed that gives eternal life, the living water that washes and cleanses, and much more.

15. Finally, the most powerful reason of all. God's Word is Jesus Christ Himself.

Jesus is described in the Gospel of John as the Living Word; the One who is God; the One who existed with God before the beginning of time; and He is the One by whom all things were created.

We do know that Jesus gained total victory over Satan on behalf of all humanity. So, when we speak the Word of God on behalf of our young people, we are actually speaking Jesus into their lives. We are bringing Him into their situations and engaging Him in their crises. Dear friend, Jesus does expect us as believers to speak His Word and use His name to enforce the victory He has already won for us.

When we speak the Word of God on behalf of our young people, we are actually speaking Jesus into their lives.

More Hope Anchors

God's unfailing love. The love of God is a powerful and secure anchor of hope for our young people. His love for them will never change. They can never go where His love cannot reach them. God's love is so great that it caused Him to pay the highest price, the life of His Son, Jesus, in order to redeem humanity out of the bondage of sin. That includes us and the young people for whom we are keeping hope alive.

The cross. Another secure anchor is the divine exchange that Jesus accomplished upon the cross through His sacrificial death. On the cross He took every curse of sin upon Himself so that we might pass from under every curse and enter into God's blessings. He shed His precious blood for us, and in the cross and His shed blood there is the power for salvation, deliverance, healing and victory over every work of the devil.

God's faithfulness, mercy and grace. We also have God's faithfulness, His mercy and His grace that are released to us through Jesus as secure anchors for our hope. Actually, all that God is and all that God does for us are unfailing anchors. Never forget that the Almighty, the Most High God, is a God of Hope.

Some Hope Mixers

We mentioned earlier that hope needs to be mixed with faith to produce results. In addition to faith, there are other qualities or attitudes that must be mixed with hope.

Obedience. Faith and obedience go hand in hand, so hope must also be mixed with our obedience to God's Word. As Jesus' mother said when He was about to perform His first miracle of turning water into wine at the marriage feast in Cana, "Whatever He says to you, do it" (John 2:5 NKJV).

Our obedience gives us the Bible right to challenge disobedience in our offspring and the young people that God has entrusted to us. Second Corinthians 10:6 speaks of being ready to punish all disobedience once our obedience in complete.

Perseverance. Hope needs a never-give-up attitude. Romans 8:25 says, "But if we hope for what we do not see, we eagerly wait for it with perseverance" (NKJV).

Like obedience, perseverance is birthed out of love. "It [love] always protects, always trusts, always hopes, always perseveres" (1 Corinthians 13:7).

One key area in which we need to persevere is in the continual speaking of faith-filled words of hope even when the circumstances and conditions are contrary.

Hebrews 10:36 gives this admonition: "You need to persevere so that when you have done the will of God, you will receive what he has promised."

We will receive what God has promised once we persevere in doing His will. My fellow Hopekeeper, He has promised us the deliverance of our sons and daughters, and other young people, out of the hand of the enemy. We can rest assured that He will do it, for His promises are sure.

The sacrifice of thanksgiving and praise. This hope mixer is a real sacrifice because it runs against the grain of our natural inclination when things are not going well. Our praise and thanksgiving prepare the way for the realization of our hope, so let us offer it up to God even before we see the manifestation of what we are hoping for. "He who sacrifices thank offerings honors me, / and he prepares the way / so that I may show him the salvation of God" (Psalm 50:23).

Be Ready To Defend Your Hope

The Bible says that we must be ready to give a reason for the hope we have within us. (See 1 Peter 3:15.) Do you know the first person to whom we will have to give an account? Ourselves! And we will have to give it not only once, but many times. Our own thoughts will sometimes rise up and question our hope.

Here is how to give a reason for and defend your hope. Have in your spirit a clearly formed image or picture of what the fulfillment of God's Word in your teenager's or young adult's life looks like. It is like having a before and after photo. But it is the "after" photo that you need to really focus on. Do not allow the image in that photo to depart from before your eyes. When circumstances (the present reality as shown in the "before" photo) challenge your hope, just hold up that "after" photo in your spirit. Then use hope-filled words to speak forth what you see with your eyes of faith.

Do you remember how the Psalmist David spoke to his soul in order to keep his hope alive?

> Why are you cast down, O my soul?
> And why are you disquieted within me?
> Hope in God;
> For I shall yet praise Him,
> The help of my countenance and my God. (Psalm 42:11 NKJV)

You will need to speak those same words to yourself over and over again as an anchor for your soul.

Let's end this chapter with praise and thanksgiving to God for being the anchor of our hope.

Heavenly Father, we bless your great and mighty name. We take pleasure in praising you as the God of hope. How we rejoice in knowing that you have given us the ability to hope in you. Thank you for the promise that when we put our hope and trust in you, we will never be put to shame. Hallelujah. Amen.

APPLICATION POINTS
FOR
THE ANCHOR OF OUR HOPE

1. In your own words explain the relationship between faith, hope and love.
2. In which of these three areas do you need to grow the most? You cannot do it in your own strength, so ask the Lord to increase your capacity in that particular area.
3. What makes Biblical hope different from wishful thinking?
4. Write a personal action plan of how you intend to keep your hope anchored as you battle for your son/daughter and other young people that are in crisis. Be specific.
5. Describe the picture that God has helped you to develop of what the fulfillment of His Word looks like in your teen or young adult's life. Keep that image in front of you when you pray for him/her. This image may change as you read through the book, especially when you start applying the strategies in Part II. Adjust the image as often as necessary.

Chapter Five

Our Creative Power and Ability

"T he Word of God conceived in the human spirit, formed by the tongue, and spoken out of the mouth becomes creative power that will work for you."[1]

My life has not been the same since the day I first read these words. I embraced them with everything within me, regretting that I had not found them earlier, but determined nevertheless to live by the principle from then on. I eventually realized that what I had discovered was God's design for all human beings.

This ability that God has given us to release creative power by the words of our mouths is perhaps the most important principle for bringing about God's miraculous breakthrough in the lives of our young people.

I said in an earlier chapter that God would not have given us the children He did or brought the young people that He did into our sphere of influence if He did not also give us what it takes to help them.

Here you have it. God put His creative power and ability in each of us, and designed each of us to express it in a unique way to meet the particular need of each one that He has entrusted to us. We often feel helpless in times of crisis, but in reality we are not. We have the God-given ability to speak forth His Word in faith as creative power for change.

Proverbs 18:21 says, "The tongue has the power of life and death." This means that, depending on what we say, the words of our mouth can kill or give life, destroy or create. We make the choice by the kind of words we speak. When we learn to use words properly, we are able to use them to destroy the undesirable or evil things that are contrary to God's will for our lives. Conversely, we can use them to produce the good that He intended for us to experience.

For many of us this will require some retraining because we have been trained to use words negatively all of our lives. Often, without even being aware of it, we use words that work against us rather than for us.

Created to Operate Like God

The ability to use words to release creative power is the unique privilege granted by Almighty God to His human offspring. No other creature has this ability. It is the ability of God Himself that He imparted to us when He made human beings in His image and likeness.

We have the God-given ability to speak forth His Word in faith as creative power for change.

God is Spirit, so to have been created in His image and likeness does not mean that we have a physical resemblance to Him. It means that we share God's nature, essence, and moral character, and that He created us to operate like Him.

And how does God operate? He operates by faith, using His words as containers to carry and release His faith. Since Jesus is the Living Word of God, He is the Word that is released as creative power when God speaks. And He is the same yesterday, today and forever. (See John 1:1-3 and Hebrews 13:8.) He is, therefore, the same creative power and energy that is available to us today.

When we read about creation in the first chapter of the book of Genesis, one of the first things that stands out is that God accomplished His work of creation by speaking. We see Him using the power of His Word to create the manifestation of what He desires. Eight times in that account we read the words: "And God said." We also read that each time God spoke, whatever He said was so.

In case we missed this in Genesis, God made sure to tell us elsewhere in the Scriptures that it is by His Word that He created everything.

Psalm 33:6 tells us, "By the word of the LORD were the heavens made, their starry host by the breath of his mouth." And in Hebrews 11:3 (NKJV) we have this statement: "By faith we understand that the worlds were **framed** by the word of God, so that the things which are seen were not made of things which are visible" (emphasis added).

Being "framed" usually carries a negative connotation. But when it comes to the Word of God it is all positive. We want to "frame" our young people with the Word of God spoken from our mouths. That's right. We want to use the Word of God to "frame" them or, in other words, to define their destiny and set boundaries for their lives.

God so wants us to operate like Him that He has given us both His Living Word, Jesus, and His written Word, the Bible. Do you see the amazing opportunity God has given you to function like Him? The creative potential that God has invested in you is indeed vast. I believe that deserves our praise. Hallelujah! Praise you, Lord!

These words spoken by Jesus to His disciples assure us of our creative ability and confirm the principle by which it works:

> …If you have faith as small as a mustard seed, you can say to this mountain, 'Move from here to there' and it will move. Nothing will be impossible for you. (Matthew 17:20b)

> Therefore I say to you, whatever things you ask when you pray, believe that you receive them, and you will have them. (Mark 11:24 NKJV)

This is the principle. We will have what we say as long as we believe in our hearts that what we say will come to pass. Never forget this principle! The restoration we are seeking for our young people depends on it.

Also, be aware that the principle works the same way in the positive and in the negative, for good or for evil. Of course, God intended us to use this ability for good. But Satan has corrupted it and trained us to use it for evil even against our own selves. We need to set a watch over the words of our mouth.

Activating and Releasing Creative Power

Now that we understand the special endowment of creative ability we received from God, our Creator and heavenly Father, let's explore how to activate and release the power or force within that ability.

The statement I quoted earlier is worth repeating. "The Word of God conceived in the human spirit, formed by the tongue, and spoken out of the mouth becomes creative power that will work for you." We need to see how it applies to the strategies for restoring our young people.

We will have what we say as long as we believe in our hearts that what we say will come to pass.

The divine intervention strategies that we will be presenting in Part II all share one common characteristic—they are constructed from the Word of God and dependent on our giving voice to them. These strategies are spiritual battle strategies and, as you will see in the next chapter, the Word of God is your "sword." Ephesians 6:17 calls it the "sword of the Spirit."

To be of any use in battle, a sword has to be drawn. The written Word of God becomes our drawn sword only when we speak it forth. Jesus illustrated this when He was tempted by the devil after His forty-day fast in the wilderness. In each instance, Jesus defeated him by speaking forth God's Word concerning the particular temptation. For example, when tempted to command stones to become bread, He declared, "It is written: 'Man does not live on bread alone, but on every word that comes from the mouth of God'" (Matthew 4:4). Let's follow Jesus' example and use the same strategy against the devil in this battle for our young people.

Here are some key points for activating and releasing the creative power that God has invested in us.

1. God's Word must first be conceived in our spirits. This involves hearing and reading the Scriptures so that the Word produces faith in us to believe and appropriate what it says is ours, and to believe that what it says is truly applicable to our circumstances. (See Romans 10:17.) It was by this process that the Virgin Mary

conceived the Word of God spoken to her by the angel concerning her giving birth to Jesus. The Word she conceived in the womb of her spirit became flesh—Jesus Christ. (See Luke 1:28-38; John 1:14.)

2. When we conceive the Word of God in our spirits, it then programs our hearts (the spiritual heart) with faith-filled and hope-filled words. Words reflecting those inner images of faith and hope are then formed on the tongue. The tongue, which is otherwise hard to tame, as James 3:6-8 tells us, eventually becomes trained and subject to a heart that is filled with God's Word.

3. Finally, according to Matthew 12:34, the mouth speaks out of the overflow of the heart. It speaks forth the faith-filled and hope-filled words that have been programmed in our hearts and formed on our tongues. As electricity is released by the flick of a switch, our speaking is the act that releases faith to generate creative power.

This process of getting the Word of God inside our hearts and seeing the manifestation of our faith-filled words takes time. It is not instant, so be diligent. Keep hearing and speaking the Word, and keep your hope alive.

More Than Vain Repetitions

The process we have just described is the process by which we get the Word of God to abide, remain, and continually live in us.

> If you live in Me [abide vitally united to Me] and My words remain in you and continue to live in your hearts, ask whatever you will, and it shall be done for you. (John 15:7 AMP)

Speaking forth the abiding Word of God is vital to the process of divine intervention. The abiding Word is effective only when we are in living union with it—when it has become part of us. That is what makes our expressions of it more than vain or empty repetition. When we speak forth an abiding

Word, we are speaking forth God's life and creative power that is within us.

The strategies that bring about divine intervention involve expressing the Word of God in different forms, such as in prayers, decrees, declarations, and affirmations. But if the Word of God is not formed in us, these expressions will not produce the intended results. Nevertheless, speaking the Word of God even when it is not yet formed in us is better than not speaking at all, or speaking negative words. Since it is God's Word that is being expressed, we would still be releasing some degree of creative power. We would be operating below our God-given potential and ability, but it is a starting point.

The strategies that bring about divine intervention involve expressing the Word of God in different forms.

Why not go all the way? Let's not fail to use the ability and power that God has given us. We will use it to destroy the works of Satan in our young people's lives and to cut off those things that need to be removed. Then we will use it to produce the good things for the fulfillment of God's plan for their lives.

Accomplishments of the Spoken Word

Since we are learning about the creative ability and power of the Word of God, I believe it will encourage us to know some of what it accomplishes when it is released in faith on our young people's behalf.

Regardless of the strategy or form in which we use the Word of God, we can expect at least these results in our young people:

1. A transmission of hope from our hearts to theirs.
2. The softening of the hard places in their hearts.
3. The watering and activation of dormant seeds of righteousness within them.
4. The shining of light into the dark places of their souls.
5. The cutting away of evil from their hearts.
6. God's angels taking heed to God's Word that has been spoken in faith and then taking action to fulfill it.

7. God's grace, mercy, power and love released as covenant blessings.
8. The establishment of new laws to govern their lives, based on God's will and intention for them that is already settled in the heavens.
9. Restraining the advance of evil in their lives.
10. The overthrow of Satan's plans, schemes and assignments.

Speaking prophetically about Jesus, Isaiah 11:4b in the Amplified Bible says, "He shall smite the earth and the oppressor with the rod of His mouth, and with the breath of His lips He shall slay the wicked." The Word of God released in faith from your mouth has the same power over the works of Satan.

First Corinthians 3:9 (KJV) tells us that we are laborers together with God. When we release our creative power and ability by speaking His Word, we show our cooperation with Him and honor our side of the covenant He has made with us. May we be faithful to this awesome privilege and opportunity.

I encourage you to make this your prayer of commitment:

Lord, as of this day, I purpose in my heart that my mouth will be used as an instrument of your power. You said to your prophet Jeremiah that you would make your Word in his mouth fire. Lord, be it unto me according to this Word. You also said that your Word is like a mighty hammer that smashes rock to pieces. Like Moses, I ask that your Word in my mouth will descend like dew, like showers on new grass, and like abundant rain on tender plants. Let your Word that goes forth from my mouth be a creative life force in the hearts of our young people, and as a mighty weapon against the forces of darkness. Thank you, Lord, that your Word will not return without accomplishing what it is sent to do. In Jesus' name. Amen. (Jeremiah 5:14, 23:29; Deuteronomy 32:2; Isaiah 55:11)

APPLICATION POINTS
FOR
OUR CREATIVE POWER AND ABILITY

1. Have you been using the creative power and ability that God has invested in you in a positive or in a negative way? What changes do you need to make?
2. Review the process by which the Word of God is activated and released as creative power.
3. What steps do you need to take to ensure that your expressions of God's Word are more than mere repetitions?
4. What are three of the results that the Word of God will accomplish in our young people's lives?

Chapter Six

The War, the Weapons and the Battlefield

The subject of warfare weapons may be new and somewhat daunting. However, there is no need for alarm or concern. We are talking about spiritual, not physical realities. What we will be dealing with are the spiritual weapons for the war that Satan is waging against God and against every human being.

For many of us the understanding we have of who God is does not include His attribute as a warrior. The Scriptures tell us, however, that "The LORD is a man of war" (Exodus 15:3 KJV). God Himself is actively engaged in spiritual warfare and so are we.

The Nature of the Warfare

This battle has both a spiritual and a legal dimension. First, let's look at the spiritual dimension.

As God's offspring, humanity is both the object of and participants in a war that is raging in the spiritual realm. We refer to this as a spiritual war or spiritual warfare, but it is not to be confused with what people call religious wars. We are not talking about war against our fellow human beings.

Satan, the devil, or Lucifer as he is also called, is the archenemy of God. He hates God and he hates us too, for we are God's treasured family of human offspring. Satan knows he is no match for God, so he goes after the thing that is dearest to God's heart. Of course that is us. Satan is therefore as much our enemy as he is God's.

In a sense, every human being steps into a spiritual war zone from the moment of conception. God, our Father, created us to express His glory on the earth, and Satan is determined, at all costs, to stop us from doing so.

But praise God that through His death and resurrection, Jesus has defeated Satan and all powers of evil. When we by faith enter into a covenant relationship with Jesus, we participate in His victory over Satan and his forces. As Romans 8:37 tells us, we are more than conquerors through Christ Jesus.

There is also a legal side to this battle because of how God operates. Although God is not legalistic, He relates to humans on the basis of laws and covenants. These laws and covenants are for our good, but when we violate them we give Satan legal ground to use them against us.

In this battle to see our sons and daughters and other young people set free from bondage, we need to know the authority that Jesus has recovered for us and how to use it against Satan. As parents we also need to know the areas in which we, our ancestors, and our children might have violated God's laws and given Satan legal access to operate.

In this battle, our focus must always be on Almighty God and on His Word.

What this means is that the battle will involve some legal proceedings in the spiritual realm. As in the natural realm, our success depends on knowing our rights and knowing how to plead our case. In the chapter on Supplementary Strategies, we will provide further insight into the strategy of pleading our young people's case in the courts of heaven.

Know Your Focus

There is something extremely important to remember in this warfare. Our battle is against Satan and his forces of darkness, but neither they nor the crisis they produced should be the focus of our attention. God promises to keep in perfect peace those whose minds are stayed on Him. (See Isaiah 26:3.) In this battle, our focus must always be on Almighty God and on His Word. We must be God-focused at all times.

Spiritual Weapons for a Spiritual War

How does the Bible describe this spiritual battle in which we are engaged and the weapons with which we fight?

We have these two very clear descriptions of the war:

> We are human, but we don't wage war with human plans and methods. (2 Corinthians 10:3 NLT)

> For we are not fighting against people made of flesh and blood, but against the evil rulers and authorities of the unseen world, against those mighty powers of darkness who rule this world, and against wicked spirits in the heavenly realms. (Ephesians 6:12 NLT)

To summarize, we are humans, but we are not fighting against people. Our enemy in this warfare is satanic forces that have different levels of authority and are called by different names. They are spirit beings that carry out their evil work on the earth by controlling, influencing, possessing, and corrupting the hearts and minds of human beings.

And what about the weapons for this warfare?

Later on in these same passages of Scripture, we also find out about the battle gear and weapons for this war.

> Therefore put on the full armor of God, so that when the day of evil comes, you may be able to stand your ground, and after you have done everything, to stand. Stand firm then, with the belt of truth buckled around your waist, with the breastplate of righteousness in place, and with your feet fitted with the readiness that comes from the gospel of peace. In addition to all this, take up the shield of faith, with which you can extinguish all the flaming arrows of the evil one. Take the helmet of salvation and the sword of the Spirit, which is the word of God. And pray in the Spirit on all occasions with all kinds of prayers and requests. With this in mind, be alert and always keep on praying for all the saints. (Ephesians 6:13–18)

> For the weapons of our warfare are not carnal but mighty in God for pulling down strongholds, casting down arguments and every high thing that exalts itself against the knowledge of God, bringing every thought into captivity to the obedience of Christ, and being ready to punish all disobedience when your obedience is fulfilled. (2 Corinthians 10:4-6 NKJV)

The Weapons and the Battlefield

From the last passage we get a general description of the weapons and the battlefield. The weapons for this battle are not the weapons that the world uses; that is, they are not carnal. Rather, they are God's mighty weapons, and His divine power is what makes them effective.

The battlefield in which this war is fought is the mind. In this battlefield the targets of our attack are called strongholds. These strongholds are established through the influence and activities of those forces described in Ephesians 6:12—"rulers...authorities...powers of this dark world and... spiritual forces of evil in the heavenly realms."

Strongholds manifest themselves as arguments, things that exalt themselves above God, thoughts, and patterns of thinking that promote self-will and independence from God rather than obedience to His ways. Our objective is to pull down every stronghold, demolish and destroy them so that the mind is open to receiving and acting upon the Word of God. Ultimately, our objective is to conquer every rebellious thought in order to bring about obedience to Christ. We start with our own minds so that we are free to perceive and receive truth, cooperate with God, and attain victory for our young people.

Warfare Weapon #1: Obedience

One would not readily think of obedience as a warfare weapon either in the natural or the spiritual realm, so it is often overlooked. However, from Second Corinthians 10:6 we get to understand that it is. How does it work? When we as parents are living in obedience to the Lord, we are in a better position to fight against the strongholds that Satan has erected in the minds of our grown children to keep them in bondage.

Verse six says that our obedience must first be fulfilled or complete. First, we must be willing and ready to destroy the strongholds of our own minds, and then we must follow through with sincere repentance before God for our own rebellion and disobedience against Him.

Our prayers for our offspring to turn from living in rebellion against God will be effective only if we have first turned. The old saying, "Do as I say, but not as I do" doesn't work any longer.

We also cannot forget that it was Jesus' humility and obedience that accomplished redemption for all of God's offspring. Adam's disobedience brought sin upon the entire human race, but Jesus' obedience brought humanity back into right standing with God.

Because one person disobeyed God, many became sinners. But because one other person obeyed God, many will be made righteous. (Romans 5:19 NLT)

Our obedience works in much the same way. As we follow in Jesus' steps, we too will live in obedience to God and exercise our God-given authority over the satanic forces that are seducing our offspring. Our obedience will work to bring about their restoration through ways and means that are beyond our imagination.

Warfare Weapon #2: God's Spiritual Armor

Based on Ephesians 6:13-18, we see that there are seven parts to the armor with which God has equipped us for this warfare. Thinking of a Roman soldier dressed for battle in ancient days has helped me to remember the parts of this spiritual armor. You might also find that image helpful.

1. The helmet of salvation covering the head (mind, thoughts, eyes and ears).
2. The breastplate of righteousness covering the heart and emotions.

3. The belt of truth firmly girding the waist and covering the loins.
4. Shoes of peace covering the feet and preparing the way for the gospel.
5. The shield of faith in hand to deflect and extinguish the flaming darts of the enemy.
6. The sword of the Spirit which is the Word of God proceeding from the mouth.
8. Finally, the Apostle Paul adds prayer which is not usually considered part of the armor, but is actually a vital part.

Prayer: A Multi-Dimensional Force

We cannot afford to be stuck with narrow or traditional concepts about prayer. Prayer is much too critical for our victory in this warfare. It is, therefore, important that we know how to pray and not miss any of its vital dimensions.

Let us review the Apostle Paul's final directive in his instructions for putting on the armor of God. "And pray in the Spirit on all occasions with all kinds of prayers and requests. With this in mind, be alert and always keep on praying for all the saints" (Ephesians 6:18).

Did you notice the level of detail that he provides in this one verse?

- Pray in the Spirit.
- Pray on all occasions.
- Pray with all kinds of prayers.
- Be alert in prayer.
- Always keep on praying.

Pray in the Spirit. To pray in the Spirit means above all that we allow the Holy Spirit to lead and guide us in prayer—directing us in the when, what and how. Our natural inclination is to pray based on our human insights and understanding, but we are limited at best. God has therefore given us His Holy Spirit to help us. He has unlimited wisdom, knows the mind of God and is able to pray accordingly. When we pray in the Spirit, we pray according to the will of God and with the power of God. (See Romans 8:26-27.)

The Word of God is Spirit, so praying in the Spirit requires praying the Word of God. It also means using the language God gives us when we receive the baptism of the Holy Spirit with the evidence of speaking in other tongues. When we pray in an unknown tongue, our spirit speaks directly to God. We allow the Holy Spirit to pray and minister through us and on our behalf. We bypass our understanding, and we confound the enemy by speaking the mysteries of God. This is one of the ways that the Spirit of God helps us in prayer and reveals hidden things to us. (See Romans 8:26-27, 1 Corinthians 14:2, 14-15.)

Prayer is also our channel through which divine military intelligence is transmitted to us. By praying in the Spirit, we receive ongoing instructions from our Commander in Chief, Jesus Christ, and remain in tune with Him.

Prayer is the battle itself, for it is through prayer that we become actively engaged in spiritual warfare.

Christians who know about the sword of the Spirit tend to speak of the whole Bible as being the sword. More accurately, however, the Bible is more like the armory where the swords are stored. The Holy Spirit knows what is in the armory because He designed it. As we understand from 2 Timothy 3:16, all Scripture is given by inspiration of the Holy Spirit. Our battle directives from headquarters come through Him. He shows us where the swords are in the armory; tells us which ones to use in which situations; and trains us to use them offensively and defensively.

Pray on all occasions. I am sure you are familiar with the customary occasions for prayer and places of prayer: church, home, morning, night, mealtime, during times of illness or other crises. How about the occasions on which this spiritual warfare requires us to pray? We need to pray as we prepare and get dressed for battle. In fact, we put on God's armor by prayer, and it is through prayer that we keep the parts of the armor functional.

Prayer is not only a means of preparation for battle. Prayer is a battle strategy and a warfare weapon. Prayer is the battle itself, for it is through prayer that we become actively engaged in spiritual warfare.

Pray with all kinds of prayers. Versatility is essential in battle. In the natural, soldiers must be skilled in different warfare tactics. It is no different in this spiritual battle. As soldiers of the Lord Jesus Christ, we must know how to pray (fight) with the different kinds of prayer. The different modes or kinds of prayer include prayers of adoration (praise and worship), thanksgiving, petition and supplication (general and specific requests for oneself and others). While we never graduate from these kinds of prayer, for us to attain victory in the lives of our young people, we need to be engaged in intercessory prayer.

Intercession simply means to "go between" or "stand in the gap" between people or circumstances and God. In intercessory prayer our focus shifts from ourselves to the needs and interests of others, and we pray what is on God's heart, not ours. We experience yet another shift in intercessory prayer when we not only speak to God, but we make declarations and decrees on His behalf concerning people and circumstances to superimpose His prophetic will and purposes over those of the devil.

Constancy in prayer is the key to victory in this battle. We cannot wait for a crisis or emergency to pray.

Jesus is our Chief Intercessor in heaven, but God is looking for intercessors on the earth who will act as Jesus' delegated authority to see heaven's will carried out in the earth. (See Romans 8:34 and Isaiah 59:16.)

Be alert in prayer. This instruction requires us to be in a state of watchfulness, not only while in prayer, but over our lives in general. We cannot entertain lifestyles that will compromise our effectiveness as God's warriors. We need to live above reproach, leaving no room for the accusations of the devil.

Being alert in prayer requires that we be mentally alert and vigilant. One of the enemy's strategies against our prayer lives is to lull us into a state of slumber (prayerlessness), or drowsiness so that we are unable to concentrate or stay awake during times of prayer. One way to fight against his strategy is to ensure that your body is well rested, and to spend time in prayer when you are most alert physically.

Always keep on praying. Constancy in prayer is the key to victory in this battle. We cannot wait for a crisis or emergency to pray. We must "pray without ceasing" (1 Thessalonians 5:17). Are you thinking that this is impossible? Well it is not. Since God's Word says this is what we are to do, it must be attainable. Here is something to keep in mind: Your prayers do not always have to be audible or lengthy, neither do they have to take the same form or be restricted to set times or designated places. On some occasions quick telegraphic prayers are all that are needed, and they are just as effective.

Faith and Love Are Essential

Concerning the armor of God, the prayer armor, and the other spiritual weapons, it is important to know that they work only by faith through love. The genuine, sincere love of God must be the basis from which we operate in order for our faith to work. As Galatians 5:6 in the King James translation tells us, "faith…worketh by love."

What does this mean? Before we start trying to engage in spiritual warfare, we have to be sure that there is no unforgiveness or anger in our hearts toward anyone. This is not a simple thing.

It is easy for us to be offended by some of the things our own teens and young adults have done—even by the pain they might have caused the family. But we cannot hold it against them, for if we do, we will not have confidence before God. Satan will not take us seriously either, for he will know that he has a stronghold in our lives.

When Jesus said in Mark 11:23-24 that if we do not doubt in our hearts we can have the things we say and ask for in prayer, He added another condition that is often overlooked: "And when you stand praying, if you hold anything against anyone, forgive him, so that your Father in heaven may forgive you your sins" (Mark 11:25). Forgiveness is mandatory for effective spiritual warfare, and it must be done quickly.

I trust that what we have covered so far has helped you to better understand the nature of the spiritual battle that is raging for our teens and young adults that are in crisis. In the next chapter we will continue to explore the weapons used in this warfare.

APPLICATION POINTS
FOR
THE WAR, THE WEAPONS AND THE BATTLEFIELD

1. How has your understanding of spiritual warfare been affected by what you have read in this chapter?
2. In what way has the reality of spiritual warfare changed your perspective on the solution to our young people's crisis?
3. What action do you need to take to change the approach you have been using in trying to change your teen or young adult?
4. Can you identify any strongholds in your mind that you need to demolish? How about in the mind of the teen or young adult with whom you are involved?
5. Take action against enemy strongholds by finding Scriptures that target the particular area. Pray and speak them in faith as weapons that will bring the mind into submission to the truth and to God's will.

Chapter Seven

The Weapons of Our Warfare

The last chapter provided an overview of the background and the nature of the war in which we are engaged. We are engaged in spiritual warfare, which simply means that we are contending with unseen forces of darkness, not against physical opponents. In this battle we are using divine weapons, methods and strategies—not those of the world. The chapter also identified two of the weapons that are essential in this battle: our obedience and God's armor.

Now, we will complete our inventory of weapons by identifying eight other essential weapons.

The Blood of Jesus

If you are not familiar with the Scriptures, you may be wondering, *How can blood be a weapon?* But the blood of Jesus is no ordinary blood; it contains the very life of God. God's law has also established the power that operates through the blood.

One of God's fixed laws since Adam sinned is that there can be no remission or eradication of sin without the shedding of sacrificial blood. The animal that was slain in the Garden of Eden to provide a covering for Adam and Eve, and those animals slain for Old Testament sacrifices were a type and shadow of the perfect Lamb of God, Jesus Christ. His blood was shed at Calvary once and for all to pay for, pardon and remove all of humanity's transgressions against God. When we put our faith in the pardoning and purifying power of the blood of Jesus, its power cuts off from our lives all the curses resulting from disobedience.

We also need to put our faith in the protecting power of the blood of Jesus. It was the power of the blood that protected the children of Israel when the death angel swept through Egypt and struck the firstborn of every Egyptian. For all of our children, and especially our firstborn, we can hold on to Hebrews 11:28.

By faith he kept the Passover and the sprinkling of blood, so that the destroyer of the firstborn would not touch the firstborn of Israel.

Like Moses, we are also to apply the blood of our Passover Lamb, Jesus, by faith over our homes and over our young people so that the destroyer cannot touch them. The blood of Jesus is for our personal protection as well. It forms a hedge of protection around us as we engage in the battle of prayer.

In this battle we are using divine weapons, methods and stategies—not those of the world.

There is wonder-working power in Jesus' blood. Praise God that His blood has not lost its power.

How do we apply the blood of Jesus? It simply requires our confession of the power of the blood and the release of our faith by the words of our mouths. As Revelation 12:11 tells us, we overcome Satan by the blood of the Lamb and the word of our testimony.

Let's speak forth our testimony and apply the blood in prayer right now.

Lord, I believe in the power of the blood of Jesus. By faith I now apply the blood of Jesus upon everything and everyone that pertains to me. Let the blood pardon, purify and protect us, Lord. And let your blood do battle on our behalf to defeat every plan of the enemy against us and our young people. Thank you, Lord, for the saving power of the precious blood of Jesus. Amen.

The Name of Jesus

Because Jesus sacrificed His life in humility for humanity, His name became the ultimate in authority and power.

> Therefore God exalted him to the highest place
>   and gave him the name that is above every name,
> that at the name of Jesus every knee should bow,
>   in heaven and on earth and under the earth,
> and every tongue confess that Jesus Christ is Lord,
>   to the glory of God the Father. (Philippians 2:9-11)

The name of Jesus represents the person of Jesus—the One in whom the fullness of God dwells. (See Colossians 1:19; 2:9.) What does this mean for us? It means that everything we need is in the name of Jesus, including hope, restoration, deliverance, salvation and victory.

Dear one, the name of Jesus is higher and greater than the name of every kind of bondage that the enemy is using to hold our young people in captivity. There is authority in Jesus' exalted name, for He stripped Satan of all authority that Adam had given over to him, and He triumphed over Satan through the cross. (See Colossians 2:15.)

Jesus has given us authority over all the power of the devil and that authority is in His name.

> Behold! I have given you authority and power to trample upon serpents and scorpions, and [physical and mental strength and ability] over all the power that the enemy [possesses]; and nothing shall in any way harm you. (Luke 10:19 AMP)

I like the Amplified translation of this verse because it tells us that we have been given both authority and power. There is a difference. Authority is the "right" to carry out a particular action, while power is the "strength or ability" needed to carry it out. Both are essential, as one is limited without the other.

When we pray, and when we send, declare or decree God's Word in the name of Jesus, we are not merely tacking on a nice phrase.

- We are appropriating the authority that Jesus has given us.
- We are standing on the ground of the totality of who Jesus is and what He has accomplished on behalf of humanity.
- We are releasing our faith in the authority and power that are invested in the name of Jesus.

May we be bold warriors exercising our God-given authority and wielding the mighty power of God against satanic forces.

I have heard people say that soldiers and police officers provide them with a picture of their authority in Christ. However, crossing guards standing in the middle of a street provide the best image for me. Many of the crossing guards that I see in my community are older, retired men and women. Some even seem a bit frail. But I am always amazed that when they step off the curb into the street in their bright orange vests and hold up their stop signs, all traffic comes to a halt, even the biggest Mack truck. That is the kind of authority Jesus has given us. The enemy must stop when we hold up the name of Jesus, plead the power of His blood and speak forth the Word of God in faith.

When we pray, and when we send, declare or decree God's Word in the name of Jesus, we are not merely tacking on a nice phrase.

One of the powerful things about the name of Jesus is that He has names that embody the power and authority that is specific to every area of need. We see results when we call upon His name for the particular situation we are dealing with.

For the turmoil in our young people's lives, they need Jesus to be their Prince of Peace. For rebellion and waywardness, they need Him as their Good Shepherd who will lead them into paths of righteousness. For their deliverance from bondage, they need Him as the Most High God. He is also their Redeemer, and the one who fights for them as the God of battles.

When we appeal to a particular name of Jesus, we are actually putting to work on their behalf the attributes of God associated with that name.

I encourage you to get hold of a resource that will provide you with an understanding of the many names of God in the Bible. Lester Sumrall's book in the Resource List is quite helpful. When you are reading the Bible, also ask the Holy Spirit to reveal to you the name of God that is associated with the particular incident that you are reading about. You will be amazed at what you discover.

Praise and Thanksgiving

Add praise and thanksgiving to your faith in the authority that is in the name of Jesus and you have an unbeatable force! First, let's look at the weapon of praise.

Praising the Lord for the attributes associated with a particular name activates the authority, power and blessing of that name for it to start operating in the life of your offspring and others.

Did you know that praise can actually defeat an army? That is what happened when three enemy armies came against Jehoshaphat who was king of Judah at the time. Jehosophat positioned singers to go in front of his army as they went out against the enemy. Second Chronicles 20:22 says that the Lord ambushed the enemy forces and defeated them as the singers and the army began to praise God.

In Acts chapter 16, we also read about Paul and Silas singing praises while in jail. Suddenly the prison doors were opened and their chains fell off. Just imagine that: praise opening prison doors!

Praise always precedes victory! The Scripture says that we live by faith and not by sight. We also praise by faith, not by sight. We praise God even when in the natural there doesn't appear to be any reason for praise.

Psalm 149:6-9 gives us a description of this powerful weapon of praise:

May the praise of God be in their mouths
    and a double-edged sword in their hands,
to inflict vengeance on the nations

and punishment on the peoples,
to bind their kings with fetters,
their nobles with shackles of iron,
to carry out the sentence written against them.
This is the glory of all his saints.
Praise the LORD.

I think of praise as joyful warfare and the antidote for deferred hope which, as Proverbs 13:12 says, makes the heart sick. Praise has the power to break through every oppression and to lift us above our circumstances. Praise charges the atmosphere with God's presence, for He lives in the praises of His people. (See Psalm 22:3.)

When should we praise? Every day; even forever and ever, regardless of our feelings and circumstances.

I will exalt you, my God the King;
I will praise your name *for* ever and ever.
Every day I will praise you
and extol your name *for* ever and ever. (Psalm 145:1-2)

Praising the Lord is more than just saying, "Lord, I praise you." Learn to make your praise specific. For example, Psalm 150:2 says, "Praise him *for* his acts of power; praise him *for* his surpassing greatness" (emphasis added). Throughout the Psalms, especially those in the later chapters, you will find that God has provided you with a wonderful collection of praise. Someone has rightly described the book of Psalms as "a spiritual thesaurus of praise and worship." Praise is a powerful warfare weapon. Use it!

Thanksgiving goes hand in hand with praise. I realize that the last thing we feel like doing when we are in the midst of a crisis is to praise or give thanks. But it is the first thing that we actually need to do.

First Thessalonians 5:18 admonishes us that it is the will of God for us to give thanks *in* all things, not *for* all things. There is a difference.

When we give thanks in the midst of a crisis, our thanksgiving becomes a sacrifice unto God that gives us the edge in battle, for "He who sacrifices thank offerings honors me, and he prepares the way so that I may show him the salvation of God" (Psalm 50:23).

That is a powerful battle strategy right there. We prepare the way for breakthrough in the lives of our young people when we give thanks to God for their deliverance and restoration even before we see any visible change in their circumstances. In fact, I encourage you to turn many of the declarations and decrees from Part II into expressions of thanksgiving.

The Righteousness of Jesus

When we put our faith in Jesus Christ we become partakers of His righteousness. In Bible terms this is known as imputed righteousness. (See 1 Corinthians 1:30 and Romans 4:22.) This righteousness is not related to our doing (the things we do), but to our being (who we are in God's eyes). Having all sinned in Adam, we could never do enough to make ourselves righteous before God, for as the Scriptures say, "All of us have become like one who is unclean, and all our righteous acts are like filthy rags" (Isaiah 64:6). But through faith in Jesus, His perfect righteousness is freely given to us to bring us into right relationship and standing with God.

This righteousness which is of God operates on our behalf as a multifaceted warfare weapon.

- It functions as a breastplate, shield and covering. (See Ephesians 6:14; Psalm 5:12.)
- It functions as a weapon for attack and for defense. (See 2 Corinthians 6:7 AMP.)
- It produces peace, quiet and confident trust. (See Isaiah 32:17.)
- It gives guidance and direction. (See Proverbs 11:5a.)
- It works deliverance for our offspring. (See Proverbs 11:21 KJV.)
- It works deliverance for us. (See Psalm 34:17, 19.)

Satan will do his best to rob us of this weapon through our feelings. We have all had times when we do not feel righteous. But bear in mind that our righteousness is not based on how we feel but on how God sees us in Jesus Christ. Our part is to maintain our relationship with Jesus and let the blood of Jesus cleanse us continually from sin. "If we confess our sins, he is faithful and just and will forgive us our sins and purify us from all unrighteousness." (1 John 1:9)

Ministering Angels

We often hear stories of angels coming to people's aid in crisis. I believe that many of those stories are true.

Psalm 34:7 tells us that the angel of the LORD encamps around those who fear Him, and He delivers them.

Psalm 91:11 says He will command His angels concerning you to guard you in all your ways.

According to Hebrews 1:14, angels are God's servants and ours. He sends them to serve, care for, and minister to those who are to receive salvation.

The key to all of this is Psalm 103:20, which says that angels obey the Word of God or heed the voice of His Word. Angels wait to hear us speak the Word of God out of our mouths; then they act on it and help bring it to pass. They are God's "swift as wind messengers" and His "flaming fire servants."

When we pray we can also ask God to dispatch angels to withstand any satanic forces that would hinder the answer to our prayers. (See Daniel 10:10-14.)

The Power of God's Love, Mercy and Grace

I believe that this is our greatest weapon when the situation is most dismal. Regardless of how great a mess they have made of their lives, our young people can never go where God's love, mercy and grace cannot reach them.

Nothing can separate us from the love of God, so we can always rely on His unfailing love. In love, God will discipline our young people for their own good. We can take comfort in God's loving discipline as a Father, for it will bring correction to them in areas where it is needed. What God said to

King David concerning his son Solomon is also true for our young people:

> I will be his father, and he will be my son. When he does wrong, I will punish him with the rod of men, with floggings inflicted by men. But my love will never be taken away from him. (2 Samuel 7:14-15a)

We need the wisdom of God to discern which hardship in the life of our young people is the discipline of God. When God's hand is at work to correct them, we have to trust His Word that He will not take His love from them.

In addition to relying on God's unfailing love, we can appeal to His grace and mercy.

Our young people can never go where God's love, mercy and grace cannot reach them.

The grace of God is what works salvation and deliverance for us. As the Scriptures tell us, "where sin abounded, grace did much more abound" (Romans 5:20 KJV).

As we pointed out before, grace is more than unmerited favor. It is divine influence working upon a heart. God has given each of us a free will that He will not overrule. However, the work of grace upon the heart will destroy those things that produce wrong choices. As we pray for our young people, we must pray for the grace of God to be poured into their hearts.

And there will be times when all we can do is ask God to extend His mercy and hold back His judgment. Like the blind man who cried, "Jesus, Son of David, have mercy on me," let us continually seek God's mercy for our young people who are walking contrary to His ways. Ask God, according to James 2:13, for His mercy to triumph over judgment. And remember, it is as we show mercy that we will receive mercy.

Fasting

In this battle we will need to seek God for His wisdom and for the appropriate strategy in handling different situations. We seek the wisdom of God through prayer and in His Word, but fasting adds another dimension and intensifies our sensitivity to the voice of God.

Throughout the Bible we see many of God's servants setting themselves aside for a fast when faced with difficult situations. Ezra, for example, proclaimed a fast when faced with the danger that could come upon Israel at the hands of their enemies as they returned to Jerusalem.

> Then I proclaimed a fast there, at the river Ahava, that we might humble ourselves before our God to seek from Him a straight and right way for us, our little ones, and all our possessions. (Ezra 8:21 AMP)

Did you notice his reasons for calling the fast? It was to humble themselves before God by showing their dependency on Him, and to entreat Him to show them the right way that they should take, not only for themselves but for their children and their possessions. When we seek God for the "right way" to deal with our young people's crisis, He will reveal to us His strategy and the weapon that will bring us victory in each situation. As God did for Ezra and others, He will also hear and answer our prayers.

From Isaiah 58:6-8 we understand that the right kind of fasting will bring about major breakthrough for us and others. It will loose the bonds of wickedness; lift heavy burdens; free the oppressed; break yokes; bring healing; and reveal hidden things.

One mother who was very concerned about the hidden things in her daughter's life went on an extended fast, after which many things came to light. Before the fast, she had only a vague sense that something was wrong. But through the fast the actual problems were uncovered.

If your health does not allow you to fast full meals, you may give up specific foods for a set period of time. You can also do a sleep fast by praying through a night watch. How about an attitude fast? For example, fasting from fear to feast on courage, or fasting from despair to feast on hope. In this kind of fast you feast on and speak forth the Word of God related to the new attitude you are seeking to create.

The fasting strategy is not intended to bring you into bondage, so use wisdom. It is not the duration of the fast or what you fast that matters. The most important thing is for your fasting to draw you into greater union with God so you can hear and obey Him.

Crying to the Lord

One Hopekeeper called me as I was finishing my preparation on this chapter. During our conversation she very casually mentioned a comment she had made at prayer meeting that morning about crying to the Lord being a weapon of warfare. She had no idea what I was working on at the time, so I realized that the Holy Spirit was providing me with insight through her.

This is the weapon available to us when there are no words or when words are not enough. Crying to the Lord and prayer can be one and the same thing, but in some respects it goes beyond regular prayer. This kind of crying is even beyond tears. It is not weeping or screaming either. It is the outburst of a desperate heart. Strangely enough, the cry may not even be heard from the outside, but what is powerful about this weapon is that God hears our cry at any frequency. He hears even our silent cries of desperation.

This weapon is what the children of Israel used against Pharoah's bondage in Egypt. Their cry brought God on the scene! Listen to what God said when he appeared to Moses: "I have indeed seen the misery of my people in Egypt. I have heard them crying out because of their slave drivers…so I have come down to rescue them from the hand of the Egyptians" (Exodus 3:7-8).

Beloved Hopekeeper, if this weapon worked for the children of Israel, it will work for us too!

In addition to responding to our cry, God will also respond to the cry of our young people, as we see in the example of Ishmael, the son that Hagar bore to Abraham. After Abraham sent Hagar and Ishmael away, they ran out of water in the wilderness. Not knowing what to do, Hagar left Ishmael under a tree to die. But Genesis 21:17 says that "God heard the boy crying." An angel called out to Hagar and her eyes were opened to see a well of water. Let's pray for a desperate cry to arise in the hearts of our offspring and for God to hear and respond to their cry as He did for Ishmael.

Crying to the Lord is a very useful weapon, especially for someone who is new in the faith. Even for veterans, it is a valuable weapon in times of desperation and weakness. Psalm 34:17 is a favorite verse of mine. It says, "The righteous cry out, and the LORD hears them; he delivers them from all their troubles."

This weapon of crying to the Lord does not work if it is rooted in self-pity, for God does not respond to wallowing. The key to using this weapon is reaching a place of humility where we acknowledge our need for the supernatural help of God and cry to him from a sincere heart. I encourage you to read Psalm 107, which chronicles many instances in which a cry to the Lord for help brought deliverance from distress and trouble.

King David knew the power of crying to the Lord and he used it successfully against his enemies. In Psalm 18:6-19 he gives a vivid description of how the Lord responded to his cry. This passage will build up your confidence in God so I encourage you to read it also.

Lamentations 2:19 gives us the strategy for crying to the Lord: "Arise, cry out in the night, as the watches of the night begin; pour out your heart like water in the presence of the Lord. Lift up your hands to him for the lives of your children."

In Psalm 56:9 (NKJV) David said, "When I cry out to you, then my enemies will turn back; this I know, because God is for me."

Let us cry out, dear one, and see the enemies that are pursuing our offspring turn back. Amen!

Summary of Our Ten Weapons of Warfare

Here now is a summary list of the ten spiritual weapons we have identified in this chapter and the previous one.

1. Obedience.
2. The complete armor of God with its seven parts: salvation, righteousness, truth, peace, faith, the Word of God, and prayer.
3. The blood of Jesus.
4. The name of Jesus.

5. Praise and thanksgiving.
6. The righteousness of Jesus.
7. God's ministering angels.
8. The power of God's love, mercy and grace.
9. Fasting.
10. Crying to the Lord.

As we end this chapter, let's look at a passage of Scripture that will help us to catch a vision of the kind of victory we can anticipate in this battle for our young people.

It is God who arms me with strength
    and makes my way perfect.
He makes my feet like the feet of a deer;
    he enables me to stand on the heights.
He trains my hands for battle;
    my arms can bend a bow of bronze.
You give me your shield of victory,
    and your right hand sustains me;
    you stoop down to make me great.
You broaden the path beneath me,
    so that my ankles do not turn.
I pursued my enemies and overtook them;
    I did not turn back till they were destroyed.
I crushed them so that they could not rise;
    they fell beneath my feet.
You armed me with strength for battle;
    you made my adversaries bow at my feet.
You made my enemies turn their backs in flight,
    and I destroyed my foes.
They cried for help, but there was no one to save them—
    to the LORD, but he did not answer.

I beat them as fine as dust borne on the wind;
I poured them out like mud in the streets. (Psalm 18:32-42)

Praise God for the victory He gives us in Christ Jesus. Hallelujah!

APPLICATION POINTS
FOR
THE WEAPONS OF OUR WARFARE

Write a few words or a sentence that expresses your understanding of the benefit, advantage, or purpose of each of the ten spiritual weapons.

1. Obedience
2. The armor of God
3. The blood of Jesus
4. The name of Jesus
5. Praise and thanksgiving
6. The righteousness of Jesus
7. God's ministering angels
8. God's love, mercy and grace
9. Fasting
10. Crying to the Lord

Chapter Eight

God's Hopekeeper Warriors

W ho is on the Lord's side? Whom shall we send? Who will go for us?

These are the questions I hear the Spirit of the Lord asking in this hour. (See Exodus 32:26; Isaiah 6:8.) And from the far off places of crooked paths, pits and dungeons into which many of our teens and young adults have wandered, and from beneath their hard façade of invincibility, I hear another desperate cry: "Who will fight for us?"

The Spirit of the Lord is crying. The spirit of our teens and young adults in crisis is also crying, involuntarily in many instances. A cry of this magnitude must be matched not by the response of a few, but by an army of parents and others who will rise up as God's faithful Hopekeeper Warriors, saying like the prophet Isaiah, "Here am I; send me!" (Isaiah 6:8).

You may have been drawn to this book by a personal need involving your own teenager or young adult in crisis. Or it may have been the need of a friend, a relative or someone in your church or community. By now you will have recognized, however, that the crisis and the need are bigger and more complex than you initially thought. We are in the midst of a serious battle that is being fought in the realm of the spirit for the souls of a generation of young people. There is no place for bystanders in this battle. We must become actively engaged.

A Declaration of War

The curse that God put on the serpent (Satan) in the Garden of Eden after Adam and Eve disobeyed God amounted to a declaration of war and open hostility between Satan and all humanity.

> And I will put enmity
>> between you and the woman,
>> and between your offspring and hers;
>> he will crush your head,
>> and you will strike his heel. (Genesis 3:15)

Jesus was the offspring of woman that ultimately accomplished the victory of crushing Satan's head by taking back the authority Adam had given over to him. God's intent is that through our relationship with Jesus, every offspring of woman will continue to enforce Jesus' victory and God's Kingdom authority over Satan. When it comes to our children, Satan's whole aim is to seduce them, turn their hearts away from God, and keep them in rebellion and bondage so that they will never exercise the authority they are supposed to enforce over him.

There is no place for bystanders in this battle. We must become actively engaged.

It is against this background that we come to understand what our young people are up against.

Not being aware of this battle in my earlier years of parenting, I was oblivious to the pitfalls that were ahead. My thinking was that if we taught our children about God and tried our best to bring them up in the right way, then they would be fine in later years. Little did I know that we had an archenemy that was waiting to capitalize on our weaknesses and mistakes. He was, as it were, lurking at the door, waiting for an opportune moment to pounce upon them. What a rude awakening I have had!

I see a picture of what many of us parents have experienced with our children in the plunder and oppression of the children of Israel by the Midianites during the time of the judges. The Midianites would just wait until the crops the Israelites had planted sprang up then they would invade the land, destroy their crops and leave them impoverished.

These terrorist attacks by the Midianites were so cruel that the Israelites had to find hiding places in mountains and caves to protect themselves and their possessions. Many of us tried to hide our children in the church, but somehow the enemy seemed to have found them. Take heart! God raised up Gideon as Israel's deliverer, and He is even now raising us up to fight for our children's deliverance.

When the angel of the Lord appeared to Gideon he called him a mighty warrior. In this battle for our offspring God is also calling us His mighty warriors. Like Gideon we may see ourselves as anything but warriors, and certainly not mighty ones. What matters, however, is what God sees in us and what He speaks concerning us. He is saying the same thing He said to Gideon: "'The LORD is with you, mighty warrior… Go in the strength you have and save [your children] out of [the enemy's hand]. Am I not sending you?'" (Judges 6:12, 14).

God Has Equipped You with a Warrior's Spirit

The Genesis 3:15 declaration of war seems to have put women, especially mothers and their offspring, at the front line of this battle that Satan is waging against humanity. But what about the men and the fathers? On the surface, this declaration of war would appear to have overlooked them, but it has not. They are the source of the seed to which the woman gives birth. It is actually their seed that Satan is after. Therefore, men and women alike, as well as their offspring, are all targets of Satan's enmity.

God, in His unfailing love for humanity would not have allowed the enmity without equipping both men and women, fathers and mothers, with a warrior's spirit to withstand Satan's hostility.

A Word Concerning Our Men and Fathers

It is evident in many families and even in the church that there is at present a deficit of warrior men and fathers who are actively engaged in this battle. I thank God for you men who have understood and honored your responsibilities before God for your family. My question to you is, "How can you help your brothers?"

I would like to remind you of an experience that the children of Israel had in their journey from Egypt to the Promised Land. When they came to Gilead, the tribes of Reuben and Gad, and half the tribe of Manasseh asked Moses for permission to settle in these lands. The region was suitable for their livestock, so they preferred to take it as their inheritance instead of what they would receive on the other side of the Jordan River.

Moses granted their request after they made a deal with him. They would first settle their wives, children and livestock in that territory, then continue across the Jordan to help their brothers until the Lord gave them rest and they also took possession of their inheritance. Joshua succeeded Moses and led the tribes across the Jordan. Now safely across on the other side of the Jordan, these tribes that had already received their inheritance renewed their commitment to Joshua, and fight they did. (See Numbers 32; Joshua 1:12-18.)

Many fathers hold the key to the restoration of their teens and young adults whose lives are in crisis.

How does that apply to our men and fathers today? Those who are living up to their responsibilities before God in the various areas of their lives have in a sense taken possession of their inheritance and birthright in the territory God gave them. But they have a responsibility and an opportunity to help their "brothers" do likewise. The need is both vital and urgent, especially for fathers who do not understand that they are created to reflect the fatherhood of God in their responsibilities to their family, the church, and their nation.

Many fathers hold the key to the restoration of their teens and young adults whose lives are in crisis. Women and mothers have been going above and beyond the call of duty. Myles Munroe, in this statement, alerts us to the critical need for our men and fathers to take their place: "A family or nation is not in order until the father is back in position. Until men are restored to their position of fathering like the Father, the people cannot be healed."[1]

Our young people speak in what sounds like coded languages. However, if we listen carefully to what their actions, behavior and words are saying, we will hear many crying out for the love of their father or someone who would show them a father's love. Many are suffering from the perils of fatherlessness.

After an appearance on a television show along with several teens to talk about teen violence, Linda Mintle, author of *Breaking Free from a Negative Self-Image,* made this observation:

> Behind the bravado, makeup, hip-hop tattoos and dog collars were hurting kids who had no fathers in their lives… Every boy on that television set was searching for masculine identity. Each one had a father who had abandoned him. Their identities were found with the gangs and loner kids who expressed their hurt through anger and violence. As one teen explained, "Boys don't cry and whine; they get even." As they searched for connection, they found community with other lost souls.[2]

Seeing a reflection of Father-God in their earthly fathers will be a major catalyst in turning the hearts of many young men and women back to God. My prayer is that all fathers will experience in a personal way the love that their heavenly Father has for them so that they can in turn express this God-kind of love to their offspring—the kind of love that would cause them to become actively engaged in the battle for their restoration and preservation.

I realize that there is a greater tendency to privacy in men than in women. Nevertheless, I believe that God is able to break down the walls of isolation, privacy, independence, and tradition in order to stir and mobilize the hearts of men and fathers for His purposes.

These Are the Days of Elijah

It seems that in every generation God has had to renew the promise and warning that He gave through the prophet Malachi at the end of the Old Testament.

See, I will send you the prophet Elijah before that great and dreadful day of the LORD comes. He will turn the hearts of the fathers to their children, and the hearts of the children to their fathers; or else I will come and strike the land with a curse. (Malachi 4:5-6)

The Amplified Bible provides a much more graphic translation of this passage:

Behold, I will send you Elijah the prophet before the great and terrible day of the Lord comes. And he shall turn and reconcile the hearts of the [estranged] fathers to the [ungodly] children, and the hearts of the [rebellious] children to [the piety of] their fathers **[a reconciliation produced by repentance of the ungodly]**, lest I come and smite the land with a curse and a ban of utter destruction. (Emphasis added.)

In this translation we see that God is speaking directly to the estranged fathers and ungodly and rebellious children. We also see something that is critical—the reconciliation or the turning of the hearts will be produced by repentance.

O that our men and fathers would cry out to God for themselves and their "brothers," acknowledging that they have missed the mark, so that we can see the fulfillment of the blessing of this promise (turning of hearts), rather than the striking of our land with a curse.

Jeremiah 14:20-21 is a good place to start.

O LORD, we acknowledge our wickedness
    and the guilt of our fathers;
    we have indeed sinned against you.
For the sake of your name do not despise us;
    do not dishonor your glorious throne.
    Remember your covenant with us
    and do not break it.

A Conscription Call

I was awakened one morning around four o'clock by a very disturbing dream about one of my sons. As I waited on the Lord for direction on how to pray I saw in my spirit a group of men sitting on the ground sound asleep under a tree. They had arrows in their hands, but as they slept the enemy came and snatched away their arrows one by one.

The Scripture that came to mind helped me to understand that the enemy had been successful in luring away our young people because he had lulled many warriors into a state of slumber, leaving their posts unguarded.

> Behold, children are a gift of the LORD,
>> The fruit of the womb is a reward.
>
> **Like arrows in the hand of a warrior,**
>> So are the children of one's youth.
>
> How blessed is the man whose quiver is full of them;
>> They will not be ashamed
>> When they speak with their enemies in the gate.
>> (Psalm 127:3-5 NAS emphasis added)

Wanting to know what could be done about this, I asked, "What now?" The response came quickly as a one-word command: "Conscript!" Immediately, the men awoke as if in a drunken stupor, fumbling around, unaware that they had been stripped of their arrows.

I believe that in this hour an urgent call and conscription order has gone forth from heaven's headquarters to awaken our men and fathers from their slumber. They are being drafted and re-positioned at the head of the battle where God had intended them to be all along. God is looking for you, and He will not let you evade His call.

For the eyes of the LORD range throughout the earth to strengthen those whose hearts are fully committed to him. You have done a foolish thing, and **from now on you will be at war.** (2 Chronicles 16:9 emphasis added) [3]

I looked for a man among them who would build up the wall and stand before me in the gap on behalf of the land so I would not have to destroy it, but I found none. (Ezekiel 22:30)

This battle for our young people has been so intensified that God's call for Hopekeeper Warriors can no longer be an invitation or a summons; it has to be a draft order.

Men, whether or not you have a biological offspring in crisis, you have been called to battle.

I make an appeal to our men and fathers: Who you are and your God-given abilities must now be placed at the disposal of the Lord of Hosts, our Commander in Chief in this battle. Our sons and daughters are depending on you. Men, whether or not you have a biological offspring in crisis, you have been called to battle.

Now, a word of comfort and encouragement: You will not be alone on the front line. God Himself has been roused to battle and has marched out with you.

The LORD will march out like a mighty man,
    like a warrior he will stir up his zeal;
    with a shout he will raise the battle cry
    and will triumph over his enemies.
"For a long time I have kept silent,
    I have been quiet and held myself back.
    But now, like a woman in childbirth,
    I cry out, I gasp and pant." (Isaiah 42:13-14)

God will put His Spirit of travail within you and release your warrior's spirit that has been dormant. He will teach your hands to war and make you mighty men of valor. Then like King David, God's mighty warrior, may you say, "Praise be to the LORD my Rock, who trains my hands for war, my fingers for battle." (Psalm 144:1).

God's Special Grace for Women and Mothers

While God has called men and fathers to the head of the battle, He has also equipped women and mothers with special grace as warriors. Many believers in Christ, even some great leaders in God's Kingdom, will tell you that had it not been for their praying mothers they might have been destroyed by Satan, and their lives would never have turned around.

God's physical design of the woman to incubate life, to travail, and to give birth has also served her well in the spiritual sphere. As a mother, she carries within herself a supernatural secret for the deliverance of her offspring. This secret is her extraordinary capacity to travail in intercessory prayer, to fight longer and harder, and to remain hopeful long after all hope seems to be gone.

I believe that no prayer moves the heart and hand of God like a mother's prayer, as attested to by this poem paying tribute to a praying mother.

THE WARRIOR

This morning my thoughts traveled along
To a place in my life where days have since gone
Beholding an image of what I used to be
As visions were stirred, and God spoke to me

He showed me a Warrior, a soldier in place
Positioned by Heaven, yet I saw not the face
I watched as the Warrior fought enemies
That came from the darkness with destruction for me

I saw as the Warrior would dry away tears
As all of Heaven's Angels hovered so near
I saw many wounds on the Warrior's face
Yet weapons of warfare were firmly in place

I felt my heart weeping, my eyes held so much
As God let me feel the Warrior's prayer touch
I thought "how familiar" the words that were prayed
The prayers were like lightning that never would fade

I said to God "please, the Warrior's name"
He gave no reply, he chose to refrain
I asked, "Lord, who is so broken that they need such prayer?"
He showed me an image of myself standing there

Bound by confusion, lost and alone
I felt prayers of the Warrior carry me home
I asked, "Please show me Lord, this Warrior so true"
I watched and I wept, for Mother…
the Warrior – was you!
— Larry S. Clark[4] ©1993

A consequence of Eve's disobedience was that she would bring forth children in pain. We have understood the natural but not the spiritual aspect of this consequence. As a mother labors to give physical birth to her children, so she must also labor to bring about their spiritual or second birth so they can fulfill their destiny in the Kingdom of God. (See Genesis 3:16; John 3:5-7.)

Much of the crisis in the lives of our young people is designed by Satan to prevent this very thing. He wants to abort their destiny by preventing them from experiencing their second birth. By so doing, he would succeed in keeping them trapped in his kingdom of darkness and out of the Kingdom of God.

Mothers, as you kept your hope alive in the natural for a quick, safe delivery, and the birth of a healthy child, so you must now keep your hope alive for a quick, spiritual delivery. Just as in physical birth you delivered your child out of the darkness of the womb into the light of day, now that your son or daughter is grown and in trouble, God needs you to deliver him or her out of the darkness of Satan's kingdom into the light of God's Kingdom. For this spiritual delivery you have God's promise: He will not allow you to come to the moment of birth and not give delivery. And in what will be to Him as a moment, you will bring forth your child into his or her second birth; even a nation, as in the case of Zion's travail. (See Isaiah 66:7-9.)

Mothers, as you kept your hope alive in the natural for a quick, safe delivery, and the birth of a healthy child, so you must now keep your hope alive for a quick, spiritual delivery.

This is essential for Hopekeeper Moms to keep in mind. It helps to explain why their battles are often so intense, why in most instances mothers feel the greatest pain when their children go astray, and why they end up fighting the longest and hardest for their deliverance. One of my Hopekeeper partners appropriately describes the situation as "children in crisis and mothers in pain." But take heart, for not only are you a warrior, but you are a victorious warrior!

It Calls for Team Work

In the book of Judges we read the account of Deborah, Israel's first and only female judge, launching a joint military attack with Barak, the commander of Israel's army, against Sisera. As the commanding officer of Jabin, a Canaanite king, Sisera had been oppressing Israel for twenty years. But Deborah cried out to God, and in response to her cry, He gave her the strategy by which Barak would defeat Sisera. Barak decided to follow the plan, but only if Deborah went with him. In the end, Sisera was killed at the hand of a woman named Jael.

I believe this account provides us with much insight and with principles that we can apply as we go forward in battle for our young people.

As Hopekeeper Warriors we are not in this battle for personal glory. It is not about whether the glory goes to the men and fathers or to the women and mothers. All of the honor goes to God Almighty!

Insight for Women and Mothers

- God has equipped you with special grace as a spiritual warrior, but he did not intend for you to be fighting by yourselves.
- Cry out to God for men and fathers to become engaged and join you in the battle. God has already issued the conscription order. Give Him no rest until the hearts of men and fathers are turned and engaged in battle. Make your plea to God as urgent and as intense as your travail for your offspring has been.
- Mobilize yourselves in prayer for the restoration of our youth, and for men and fathers to take their place in the battle. Join a prayer group or start one for the cause. "This is what the LORD Almighty says: 'Consider now! Call for the wailing women to come; send for the most skillful of them'" (Jeremiah 9:17).
- Arise as Deborah did and take the initiative when necessary. "Village life in Israel ceased, / ceased until I, Deborah, arose, / arose a mother in Israel" (Judges 5:7).
- Even as Deborah told Barak of God's instructions, seek out the men and fathers who will help to implement God's battle plan for our young people's restoration. Make it a Barak and Deborah team!

Let's pray concerning that right now:

Now, Heavenly Father, we pray that you would awaken our men and fathers. We cry out to you, awaken them from their slumber! We ask you to anoint them with the spirit and power of Elijah. Empower them with your warrior spirit and your spirit of leadership as in the days of Nehemiah. Cause them to rise up and fight for their homes, for their families, for their wives, for their sons and daughters, for their brothers and sisters, for their nation, for your Kingdom. In Jesus' name we pray. Amen.

Insight for Men and Fathers

- The special grace with which God has equipped women and mothers does not excuse you from the battle. Do not be intimidated. Be strong and courageous. Take your place at the front line. Join the women and mothers on the battlefield and make it a Barak and Deborah team. There is grace available to you too. You will find it as you go with confidence to the throne of grace in prayer. (See Hebrews 4:16.)

- Begin to travail. Travailing is not just for women. Imitate God, your heavenly Father, even as He has roused Himself and now cries out, gasps and pants like a woman in childbirth. (See Isaiah 42:14.)

- Like the men in Nehemiah's days, hear and respond to the divine call: "Don't be afraid of them (the enemy). Remember the Lord, who is great and awesome, and fight for your brothers, your sons and your daughters, your wives and your homes" (Nehemiah 4:14b).

- Make a commitment and stick to it; for God's sake and for the sake of our young people that are in crisis. "As for me, far be it from me that I should sin against the LORD by failing to pray for you. And I will teach you the way that is good and right" (1 Samuel 12:23).

A Mighty Victorious Force for God

Men and fathers, women and mothers, united we will stand against the enemy in this battle for our young people, but divided we will fall.

> Behold, how good and how pleasant *it is*
> For brethren to dwell together in unity!
> *It is* like the precious oil upon the head,
> Running down on the beard,
> The beard of Aaron,
> Running down on the edge of his garments.

It is like the dew of Hermon,
　　Descending upon the mountains of Zion;
　　For there the LORD commanded the blessing—
　　Life forevermore. (Psalm 133 NKJV)

We are coming together as one for the purpose of receiving the blessing of God's abundant eternal life for our sons and daughters, and for a generation of young people. For this cause, the Lord is pouring out His Spirit upon us, a particular Spirit—the Spirit of grace and supplication.

And I will pour out on the house of David and the inhabitants of Jerusalem a spirit of grace and supplication. They will look on me, the one they have pierced, and they will mourn for him as one mourns for an only child, and grieve bitterly for him as one grieves for a firstborn son. (Zechariah 12:10)

Let's get in the outpouring, and in this spirit of grace and supplication that we have received from the Lord; let us cry out and fight in intercession as a mighty victorious force for God. Prayer is the battle. We fight through intercessory prayer.

Sound the alarm…!
Blow the trumpet…!
Raise the battle cry…!
Lead on into battle O warriors…! (Hosea 5:8 NLT)

APPLICATION POINTS
FOR
GOD'S HOPEKEEPER WARRIORS

1. On a scale of 1 to 10, how would you rate your current level of involvement and commitment in the battle for the restoration of your teen or young adult, and/or other young people?
2. What is stopping you from becoming more involved and committed?
3. What steps will you now take to improve your level of involvement and commitment? Ask the Holy Spirit to direct you in finding another Hopekeeper to whom you can be accountable.
4. Why is the involvement of men and fathers so essential in this battle?
5. Women and mothers who are already engaged in the battle need to guard against becoming battle worn. What precautions can they take?
6. Explore opportunities to start a new Hopekeeper support group in your community or join an existing one. (It takes only two committed individuals to start a new group.)
7. What are some of the ways that your group could get more men and fathers involved?

Chapter Nine

Preparing for Battle

O ur preparation for battle is as important as our actual participation. In fact, taking time to prepare for any endeavor puts us in an advantageous position to succeed in whatever lies ahead. Throughout the Scriptures we see God preparing Himself and others for what was forthcoming.

At creation, the Holy Spirit hovered over the waters, the chaos and darkness that covered the face of the deep before God started His creation work. (See Genesis 1:2.) Moses prepared 80 years for the last 40 years of his life in which God used him as Israel's deliverer. God's own Son, Jesus, prepared 30 years for an earthly ministry of three years.

Everything you have read up until now in this first section of the book is part of your preparatory process for being used of God to make a difference in our young people's lives. Now we will be advancing that process with seven specific preparation steps.

Steps two, three and four are unique to Hopekeeper parents, but even if you are not a parent, you will want to familiarize yourself with them. Doing so will prepare you to help parents that you may encounter. You may also pray for the parents of the young people with whom you are involved for them to become aware of the need to take these preparation steps.

Here is something to keep in mind. This is not a typical preparation process which, once done well, does not have to be repeated. What we are about to undertake are initial preparatory steps. We will need to incorporate some of them into our lifestyles going forward.

Preparation Step #1: Right Standing With God

The first thing to do in preparing ourselves for battle is to ensure that we are restored into right standing or relationship with God, our heavenly Father. This is necessary because the sin nature inherited from Adam and Eve, and our own personal sins have separated us from God.

There are two primary benefits to be gained from this first step.

1. Being in right relationship with God brings us into covenant with Him. This is extremely important because, as we pointed out in the first chapter, the divine intervention strategies that you will be applying operate through a covenant partnership. If you are a parent, God's covenant with you extends to your offspring and descendants.

> As for me, this is my covenant with them, says the LORD. "My Spirit, who is on you, and my words that I have put in your mouth will not depart from your mouth, or from the mouths of your children, or from the mouths of their descendants from this time on and forever," says the LORD. (Isaiah 59:21)

> He remembers his covenant forever, / the word he commanded, for a thousand generations. (Psalm 105:8)

> Know therefore that the LORD your God is God; he is the faithful God, keeping his covenant of love to a thousand generations of those who love him and keep his commands. (Deuteronomy 7:9)

> From Acts 2:38-39 we also understand that God's promise is for us and our children and all who are far off. I take this to include

even the generations that are yet to come from our family line. The experiences of many in the Bible such as Noah, Abraham, Rahab the harlot, Cornelius, Lydia, and the jailer in Philippi assure us that God's covenant of salvation is for whole families and households. (See Genesis 7:1, 18:19; Joshua 2:12-19; Acts 11:4-18, 16:13-15, 31-34.)

2. A right relationship with God is the prerequisite for representing Him on the earth and for using the authority He has given us against Satan. We must be joined to God through a vital relationship with Jesus Christ, so that His overcoming faith, authority and power can work through us.

I would like to pause here and deal with this vital matter on a more personal level before we go on. I have a couple of important questions to ask you. How would you describe your relationship with God? Do you know Him as your heavenly Father? If you are estranged from God, I bring you the good news of reconciliation. There is no need to remain separated any longer.

God, the Father, gave us the gift of His Son, Jesus, who shed His blood and gave His life on Calvary as payment for the sin that separates us from Him. There is only one way to be reconciled and be made right in God's sight, and that way is through Jesus Christ and by the power of His blood.

Jesus tells us in John 14:6 that He is the way, the truth and the life. No one comes to the Father except through Him. There is nothing we can do, dear one, to save ourselves from the penalty of sin or make ourselves acceptable to God. Not even our good works can help us. So if you have never accepted Jesus as Savior, I would like to give you an opportunity to come into right standing with God by receiving Jesus now.

Would you open your heart to Him and repeat this prayer for salvation?

Heavenly Father, I repent of my sins and ask your forgiveness. I accept your gift of salvation through Jesus Christ, and I now invite Him into my heart and life as my Savior and Lord. Amen.

Congratulations!

If you meant that from your heart, the relationship between God as your heavenly Father and you as His child has been restored. You have received the righteousness of Jesus, which means that God now sees you as righteous! You now have a Bible right to use the authority that Jesus Christ has given to those who believe in Him.

For your spiritual growth, training and maturity in Christ, and for ongoing support, I encourage you to connect with a community of faith where the Bible is taught, and to start fellowshipping with other believers in Christ on a regular basis.

Preparation Step #2: Repentance

This second step involves a further dimension of repentance, and is primarily for Hopekeeper parents. The first step dealt with the dimension of our personal standing with God. The purpose of this second dimension is three-fold:

1. To position or align us for answered prayers.
2. To ensure that there are no barriers between us and God, and that there is nothing to prevent Him from working on our behalf when we begin to do battle or warfare for our offspring.
3. To deal with any consequences of sin that may continue operating in our lives and in our children's lives even after we have been reconciled to God.

Some of these issues may even have had their origin in earlier generations, but they continued through the family line because no one stood before God to acknowledge the sin, repent and ask forgiveness.

The Bible refers to the consequences of sin that have resulted in patterns of weaknesses and evil predispositions being passed from one generation to the next as the "mystery of iniquity" or the "secret power of lawlessness." (See 2 Thessalonians 2:7.)

We have a Bible promise associated with this step:

If my people, who are called by my name, will humble themselves and pray and seek my face and turn from their wicked ways, then will I hear from heaven and will forgive their sin and will heal their land. (2 Chronicles 7:14)

This preparation step requires repentance before God in four areas:

1. *For ourselves.* Our children did not only inherit our physical characteristics. They also inherited our predispositions to certain patterns of sin. Our confession and repentance before God for our personal sins and areas of weakness will break the power of those patterns in our own lives and in the lives of our offspring. Whatever we free ourselves from means more freedom for our offspring.
2. *For parental shortcomings.* When we become aware of areas of past parental shortcomings, we need to acknowledge them before God and seek His forgiveness.
3. *On behalf of our family, including our children.* God laid down the pattern for this in Leviticus chapter 16, where He said that the priests were to make atonement for themselves and their household. As you will see later, the priestly responsibility of representing our children to God is one of the responsibilities that God has given to us as parents.
4. *On behalf of our ancestors.* Leviticus 26:40-44 also talks about the people confessing their sins and the sins of their fathers (their treachery against God, and their hostility toward Him) that have made God hostile toward them.

     I believe the sincere repentance of even one family member is all that God requires to start delivering a family line from the progression of ancestral bondage and curses.

As God said in Ezekiel 22:30, "I looked for a man among them who would build up the wall and stand before me in the gap on behalf of the land so I would not have to destroy it, but I found none."

We see an example of this kind of repentance being done in the Bible by Nehemiah when he heard about the trouble and disgrace Jerusalem was in because of its broken down walls. Daniel also took this same step of confessing ancestral wickedness when he was seeking an end to the Babylonian captivity of his people. I believe it would be wise for us to follow the examples of Nehemiah and Daniel.

Here are two prayers of repentance covering the four areas we have just identified.

REPENTANCE ON BEHALF OF OURSELVES, OUR FAMILY AND OUR ANCESTORS: *Our Most Holy God and Father, you who are the great and awesome God who keeps your covenant of love with those who love you and obey your commands, I appeal to your great love and mercy that you have shown us in giving your Son, Jesus, as the complete sacrifice for our sins. Like Nehemiah and Daniel, I confess to you today the sins that my people, including myself, my family and my father's house have committed against you. We have rebelled and acted wickedly towards you and have not obeyed you or followed your ways.*

I ask you to forgive all our iniquity. Let the blood of Jesus now pardon, purify and cleanse my entire family line and let it break every yoke of bondage that has come upon us because of our rebellion.

By faith in Jesus' sacrifice on the cross, I believe that we are redeemed from every curse of the enemy, and I now appropriate on behalf of myself and my offspring, even unto the generations to come, every blessing with which you have blessed us. With thanksgiving, we now receive your bless-

ing, Father, in the name of our mighty Redeemer and Savior, Jesus Christ. Amen. (Based on Nehemiah 1:5-7 and Daniel 9:4-19.)

REPENTANCE FOR PARENTAL SHORTCOMINGS:
Heavenly Father, we thank you for being the perfect Father in every way. We ask you to forgive us for not parenting our children the way you intended. Forgive us for unintentionally opposing heaven's desires for them. We repent for having imposed our will on them rather than seeking to understand your will for their lives. Forgive us, we pray, for wanting to clone them in our own image rather than molding them in the image of God. Forgive us, and cancel every word that we spoke to them in retaliation, frustration, anger and pain.

We also ask, Father, that you would forgive us for every hindrance that we have inadvertently and ignorantly put in the way of our children that has caused them them not to see and know you for who you really are, or desire to come to you. We call upon you to restore them to your perfect will for their lives. Thank you, Father. In Jesus' name. Amen.

Our repentance opens the way for the Sovereign Lord to bring good out of bad situations and turn for good what was meant for evil. Confession and repentance also build a bridge between us and the next generation, and open the way for generational and personal blessings that might have been held up to now be released.

Do not underestimate your power to make a difference as one person. You have probably heard the expression that "One plus God equals a majority." All God needs is one human agent through whom He can work on the earth. He created the entire human race through one man—Adam. He redeemed humanity through one man—Jesus. He chose one nation—Israel—to demonstrate His power and ways to the world. Has God chosen you as the one who will make a difference in your family line, or in the lives of the young people He has placed within your sphere of influence?

Preparation Step #3: Rise Above Your Grief

As parents we have bright hopes for our children, but when as teens and young adults, they end up on the wrong path; our initial response usually runs between shock, bewilderment, and anger. "Why?" "How could he/she do that?" "How could this be?" These are some of the questions that haunt our minds. But there is really no reasonable answer to satisfy us. Eventually grief sets in as the crisis worsens or is prolonged.

I have met parents and others who have not been able to move beyond lamenting what has become of a son, daughter, grandchild, or a relative. Interestingly enough, many did not recognize that they were in a state of grieving. You see, we usually associate grief with death but not so readily with lost dreams, hopes, and expectations. In reality, however, there is cause for grief when it seems that the crises in our young people's lives dash to pieces our dreams for their future, threaten to waste their potential, and destroy everything we have invested in them.

As you prepare to do battle for the restoration of your son or daughter, I encourage you to acknowledge your grief and give it the expression it needs so that you will be able to move beyond it. Cry and wail if you have to. But know that with each passing moment of sorrow you are about to rise up in strength for the battle.

Satan would want nothing more than for us to remain stuck with grief so that we never rise up to do battle against him and fight for our young people's restoration. I have learnt from experience that the longer I continue to lament my losses the longer I feel defeated. Our young people who need us to fight for them remain defeated as long as we remain in grief.

At this point you may be thinking that this is easier said than done. I understand. I also felt this way when I was stuck at that place of lamentation. But I found hope and strength in Jesus' resurrection power. The account of the death and resurrection of Lazarus in the Gospel of John chapter eleven helped me considerably. As Jesus asked Martha (and also asked me), I now ask you: "I am the resurrection and the life… Do you believe this?" (John 11:25-26). May we always receive the grace to answer as she did, "Yes, Lord…I believe" (John 11:27).

Let's believe together that we will indeed see our young people's lives restored, that one day Jesus will lovingly smile at us and say: "Did I not tell you that if you believed, you would see the glory of God?" (John 11:40). So be it, Lord Jesus!

Preparation Step #4: Release Your Offspring

This fourth step in the preparation process is also for Hopekeeper parents. It is for the release of our offspring; first, from enemy strongholds of the past that might have involved us and, second, for their release into the hand of God.

1. When we as parents are able to acknowledge to our grown children in crisis that we have contributed to some of the challenges they have been facing, it releases amazing supernatural power to help them overcome their weaknesses.

   This is not about parents being saddled with blame, nor does it negate our young people's responsibility for their choices and actions. It is about our preparing a way for God to move on their behalf through our humility and honesty. As James the epistle writer admonishes: "Confess to one another therefore your faults (your slips, your false steps, your offenses, your sins) and pray [also] for one another, that you may be healed and restored (to a spiritual tone of mind and heart)" (James 5:16 AMP).

   I realize that this is not something that parents are accustomed to doing, so it may take us out of our comfort zone. It requires courage, and the Holy Spirit will provide what we need.

2. Releasing our offspring into the hands of God benefits both us and them. It is the best place for them to be, and we can rest assured that ultimately only good will come to them as long as we leave them there. God will faithfully keep whatever we

commit into His hands, and He is able to work all things together for their good. (See 2 Timothy 1:12; Romans 8:28.)

Psalm 127:3-4 tell us that our children are a heritage, gift, and reward from the Lord, and they are like arrows in the hand of a warrior. Everything that we have, including our children, belongs to God. But we have the responsibility to be good stewards over them. I have now come to understand that the first principle of stewardship is to release and dedicate back to God what He has given us. Therefore, the first step in fulfilling our responsibility to our children is to dedicate them back to God.

Many parents follow the tradition of christening or baptizing their infants. This is good. However, dedicating or committing our children to God involves more than asking God to bless and watch over them. It also requires more than a one-time act. It calls for complete and repeated committal, especially in their older years when we are likely to start worrying about their choices and lifestyles.

We do a great disservice to God, ourselves, and our children when we do not recognize and operate on the basis of the principle that they belong to God, who is their heavenly Father. I am convinced that having this fundamental truth planted in the heart of a very young child will make a significant difference in later years.

A few years ago, prior to receiving the understanding that I now have, one Sunday morning after the church service I went to the altar for prayer concerning a major crisis in the life of one of my grown children. The very wise altar worker who ministered to me instructed me to first take the step of dedicating my children back to the Lord. I informed her that I had already done so when they were babies. But she explained to me that I needed to release them into the hands of the Lord—repeatedly give them back to Him. I followed her advice right there and almost instantly the burden was lifted from my shoulders. Since that day, whenever I start feeling overwhelmed and burdened over any of my children or grandchildren, I realize that it is time to release them once more into God's hands.

Would you take this step with me in prayer right now?

Dear Father, thank you for the gift of my children. I release, dedicate, and commit them back to you as their heavenly Father so that your will for their lives can be fulfilled. I now release _____ (fill in their names) into your hands with joy, being confident and fully persuaded that by the power and authority of Jesus' name you are able to guard, defend, and keep them from every evil. You are the Lord their Savior, and I dedicate them to you as the One who will bring about their salvation. As their parent, I also dedicate myself to you to become and to do all that you desire of me on their behalf. Thank you, Lord. Amen.

I encourage you to make a regular practice of releasing and dedicating your offspring to God.

Preparation Step #5: Fulfill Your King-Priest Responsibility

Through Jesus Christ we are made kings and priests unto God. (See Revelation 1:5-6.) This means that as Hopekeepers for our young people, we have both a kingly and a priestly responsibility before God and toward them.

Our king-priest responsibility refers to the kind of authority that God has given us to operate in the spiritual sphere. For parents, it refers to the responsibility and authority God has given us to exercise on His behalf to ensure that His purposes are accomplished in our children. Other Hopekeepers such as guardians, pastors, mentors to whom God has entrusted non-biological "children" also have this responsibility and authority for their lives.

God's intent is that men and fathers take the lead in carrying out these responsibilities. Unfortunately, many fathers are either absent, unaware, or unprepared so many women and mothers have had to fill in the gap. Let's not forget to pray fervently for God to correct this deficiency and imbalance by His conscription and turning of the hearts of our men and fathers as was expressed earlier.

What does the king-priest responsibility involve?

In our kingly function, we represent or bring God to our young people by establishing His will and kingdom in their lives on the earth as it is already established in heaven. We do this by declaring, decreeing and proclaiming God's Word over their lives. In representing God to our young people, we also reflect His love and character as their perfect heavenly Father.

Most fathers have understood the disciplinary aspect of this responsibility. Unfortunately, to the detriment of their children, many have been negligent in demonstrating other equally important dimensions of God's heart as a Father, such as His love, compassion and nurturing. It is important in carrying out the disciplinary aspects of our kingly responsibility that we do so in love and balance our actions.

Whereas in our kingly function we represent God to our young people, in our priestly function we represent them to God. We do this through prayer.

In Old Testament times, the breastplate of the garment that the High Priest wore into the Holy Place had stones with the names of the twelve tribes of the children of Israel attached to it. The intent and significance of this was that the priest would "bear the names of the sons of Israel on the breastplate of judgment over his heart…as a memorial before the LORD continually" (Exodus 28:29 NKJV).

Let's take this priestly responsibility seriously and continually bear the names of our young people before God in prayer. When we carry them on our hearts to God, He will have a way of turning their hearts to Him. If we really want to see their lives changed, we must make praying for them a top priority.

Our teens and young adults who are in trouble or are headed for trouble need divine intervention to see them through. God is counting on us to fulfill our responsibilities as King-Priest Hopekeepers, and so are our young people.

Preparation Step #6: Learn How to Walk in Faith and Expectation

This sixth step prepares us to become Hopekeepers who walk in faith and expectation. It starts with the development of our faith. We develop our faith by hearing the Word of God and getting it into our hearts.

I encourage you to start exercising your faith in small things and watch it grow. If you are someone who thinks that you have no faith, it is time to start believing Romans 12:3 which says that God has given to everyone a measure of faith. Start by using what you have. Then, once you have done that, you can ask for an increase, like the disciples who said to Jesus, "Lord, increase our faith" (Luke 17:5).

We have to be prepared to exercise the "carrying" kind of faith on behalf of our young people.

Here are three reasons why it is important for us to start using and developing our faith.

First, the exercise of our faith is what pleases God and activates His miracles. We need faith to appropriate every promise that God has given us in His Word.

Second, we cannot fight this battle on behalf of our young people without the exercise of our faith. I firmly believe that in most cases it is our faith as Hopekeepers that will carry our young people into their miraculous breakthrough. We have to be prepared to exercise the "carrying" kind of faith on behalf of our young people. This is the kind of faith that the friends of a paralytic man displayed in letting him down through a roof when there was no other way of getting him to Jesus. It was not the man's faith that Jesus saw, but his friends'. Jesus healed him on the basis of their faith. (See Mark 2:1-5.)

In various other New Testament accounts, we also see that Jesus brought healing and deliverance to children on the basis of their parent's faith. The Canaanite woman in Matthew 15:21-28, the royal official whose son was close to death in John 4:46-53, and the man whose son had an evil spirit in Mark 9:14-29 are cases in point.

Third, it is important to start using and developing our faith because we will need eyes of faith to see our young people and their circumstances as God sees them.

Our young people are not what they do, but if we do not have God's perspective we will make the mistake of using their bad choices and inappropriate lifestyles to define them. And if we only see what is on the outside, we are bound to give up in despair. We need to ask God for His vision so that we can see them through His eyes, see His mighty hand at work in their lives, and love them unconditionally through every crisis as He does.

You may think that it is impossible to ignore what you see. No one expects you to live in denial. Rather, it is all about seeing what is possible through the eyes of faith.

Some time ago I heard these two really great explanations of how faith operates:

- Faith sees the invisible, believes the incredible and receives the impossible.
- Faith acts as if a thing is so, even when it is not so, that it might be so.

That is the realm in which we want to operate. When we see through eyes of faith, then we are able to release faith-filled words to create in the visible realm what God has already established in the invisible.

As Hopekeepers we believe in victory for our young people; a victory we see at first, not with our natural eyes, but with eyes of faith. I like the translation of Hebrews 11:1 in the New Living Bible: "Faith is the confidence that what we hope for will actually happen; it gives us assurance about things we cannot see."

Faith works with expectation, so live with great expectation of seeing your offspring and other young people living victorious lives. Expect a miracle! Expect their breakthrough!

In the parable of the lost son in the Gospel of Luke, the father was able to see the son "while he was still a long way off" because he was expecting him to come home. That is expectation! (See Luke 15:11-32.)

The crippled beggar at the Temple gate in the book of Acts was expecting to receive something from Peter and John as they passed by. He got something better than money. He was made whole. (See Acts 3:1-10.)

Our hope is our expectation. Keep it alive! Continually declare Psalm 27:13: "I am still confident of this: I will see the goodness of the LORD in the land of the living."

Preparation Step #7: Be Armed and Battle Ready

Finally, preparing ourselves requires that we be armed and battle ready. We do this by clothing ourselves in the full armor of God. As I said in an earlier chapter, we put on the armor by prayer.

The armor of God works only if certain other key factors are in place. Some have been covered in this chapter and others in previous chapters. Let's do a quick check to ensure they are in place before we pray.

1. Have you brought your relationship with God into right standing through faith in Jesus Christ as your Savior?
2. Have you brought your relationship with others into good standing by forgiving them of their offenses?
3. Have you sincerely repented before God for yourself and on behalf of your ancestors and offspring?
4. Is your heart built up with an attitude of faith?

Before going on, I encourage you to take the time, go back, and deal with any area in which you feel unprepared.

Now that we are ready, let's put on our armor in prayer:

Heavenly Father, having come into right relationship with You and with others, I declare that I am strong in You and in Your mighty power. I put on Your full armor that You have provided for me, and with this armor, I stand my ground against the enemy.

I recognize that my mind is the battlefield and the target of Satan's attacks, so I cover my mind with Your powerful helmet of salvation. Thank You for protecting my mind and for giving me sound thinking.

I put on the breastplate of righteousness, which is the righteousness of Jesus Christ. Let Your righteousness guard my heart and emotions from any assault by the enemy.

Thank you, Lord, for the belt of truth. I stand firm with this belt of truth buckled around my waist. Protect me from the lies of the enemy and let my life be governed only by Your truth. And with this belt of truth, I gird up my mind and prepare for action.

I step into and stand on Your solid rock of peace, and ask that Your supernatural peace will guard my heart and thoughts.

I lift up the shield of faith against every fiery dart that Satan fires against me. Thank You for surrounding me with Your shield of victory at all times.

I take up the sword with which You have equipped me, Your holy Word. I hide Your Word in my heart and declare it boldly from my mouth to defend myself and my family, and to defeat Satan. Let me use Your Word to pierce and shatter any darkness that would seek to surround us each day.

Father, I thank You that through prayer You enable me to keep the armor in place and effective. With joy I declare that I am more than a conqueror, I am victorious and triumphant through Christ Jesus. Amen. Thank You, Jesus. Hallelujah! (From Ephesians 6:10-18, 1 Peter 1:13.)

This brings us to the end of Part I. Your faithfulness in laying the foundation for what you will be practicing in Part II will certainly pay off.

APPLICATION POINTS
FOR
PREPARING FOR BATTLE

1. Why are the reconciliation to God and the maintenance of a lifestyle of repentance so critical in this battle?
2. Ask the Holy Spirit to help you if you have not yet taken the step to be reconciled to God through Jesus Christ. If you are unsure about taking this step, I encourage you to speak to someone who will be able to answer any questions you may have and pray with you.
3. Identify any repeated patterns and cycles in your family that you know or suspect are operating in your offspring. Acknowledge them before God and ask Him to remove the curse from your family line. See the Resource List for books that will be helpful in this area.
4. Identify any personal action you need to take for each of the seven preparation steps.
   a. Coming into right standing with God
   b. Repentance
   c. Rising above grief
   d. Releasing your offspring
   e. Fulfilling your king-priest responsibility
   f. Learning to walk in faith and expectation
   g. Being armed and battle ready

PART II
DIVINE INTERVENTION STRATEGIES

"It seems God is limited by our prayer. He can do nothing for humanity unless someone asks Him to do it."

— JOHN WESLEY

"Without prayer work, all other work will have little or no permanent effect on anyone or anything."

— J. GORDON HENRY

Chapter Ten

Introducing the Strategies

Welcome to Part II. Congratulations! You have stayed the course, and now you have come to the long awaited intervention strategies.

In case you skipped over the first part of the book or some of it, I encourage you to go back and read it through completely. You will need the foundation teaching it provides in order to get the maximum benefit from this section. I know you are eager to get started on the strategies, but once you have completed the first section you will be ready to go.

Personalize Your Strategy

Be aware that the intervention strategies we will be presenting are not canned or ready-made formulas, for no two situations are exactly the same. Each one requires a different approach. Even if you are involved with more than one teenager or young adult in crisis, it is best to focus on each one individually. The underlying root of the crisis is the same, but it manifests itself differently in each life. This requires that you personalize your strategy.

Bring each teenager and young adult by name to God and pray specifically for his or her needs. To do this, you may wish to set aside specific days or times to pray for each one. You will begin to see different results as you give this kind of focus to your prayers.

Let the Holy Spirit Guide You

As you speak these prayers, decrees, declarations, confessions, and use these strategies, the Holy Spirit will highlight different things to you. Take note of what you find yourself being drawn to, and of what seems most relevant at a particular time. These are "Focal Points," and the Holy Spirit will use them to put into your hands and mouth the specific weapon you need for the particular situation, battle or crisis.

At the end of each chapter, we have provided space for you to record your Focal Points for the various strategies. Date your entry to help you track the Holy Spirit's leading over time.

In addition to using the examples in the various chapters, you will also need to inquire of the Holy Spirit and seek His wise counsel for more insight. Take whatever insights you receive and combine them with relevant examples from each chapter. We also encourage you to study and search the Scriptures for additional promises pertaining to the specific area of concern that you have for your teenager or young adult. In this way you will develop a personalized list that targets their particular circumstances.

Strategy is everything in warfare.

Satan chooses his strategies carefully and so must we.

Strategy is everything in warfare. Satan has strategies, tactics, and devices of which the Bible says we are not to be ignorant. (See 2 Corinthians 2:11.) Satan chooses his strategies carefully and so must we.

God has given us the Holy Spirit to counsel, guide and help us develop strategies that will outwit Satan. Remember, you are dealing with spiritual battles, and depending on the nature of the battle, you will need to know the particular strategy and weapons to use. You can fully rely on the Holy Spirit to reveal to you the strategy and weapon that will be most effective in a particular situation.

You may find that at certain times the Holy Spirit will have you focus on one strategy, then different ones at other times. Your number one job is to cooperate with Him by seeking His help and following His direction. Never forget that your obedience is a warfare weapon.

David was Israel's greatest warrior king, and what stands out about his warfare is that he would not go to battle until he inquired of the Lord. Often the Lord gave David explicit instructions on the strategy to follow, and David followed in complete obedience. What was the outcome? The Lord gave David victory everywhere he went. Unlike David, we are not fighting physical wars, but the principles of dependency on the Lord and obedience still apply. May we all be successful warriors like King David.

The Strategies and Their Purposes

We will be covering a total of twelve strategies in this section, starting off with strategic prayers. In a sense one could think of all the strategies as prayers or intercession. However, we have differentiated them, not only for convenience but also to distinguish the various ways in which we are using the Word of God. In some instances you may find that certain Scriptures are repeated in the examples under different chapters. That is intentional. It amounts to fighting with the same weapon in different ways.

With the prayer strategy, we are speaking God's Word back to Him based on His covenant promises and our faith in Him. We are making petition, offering praise, honor, and adoration to God. We are also engaging God in our affairs by giving Him the access He requires. And do not forget; it is through our prayers that we fertilize and soften the soil of our young people's hearts for them to respond to the grace of God.

While using the prayer strategy, we operate in our priestly authority to bring our young people to God. With the other strategies, we operate in our kingly authority of bringing the will and Word of God to them. Both go hand in hand, enabling us to shift from one dimension to the other according to the circumstances and the leading of the Holy Spirit. We start with petitioning God, but to be effective we must go on to proclaim, declare and decree His Word over each situation.

When we send, decree, declare and confess the Word of God, we are speaking prophetically concerning His will and calling it forth into our young people's lives. We are releasing creative power, blessing and hope. We are speaking life into the things we want to live and death to the things we want to cut off from their lives. We are planting seeds of righteousness in their hearts, and sending spiritual rain to cause them to grow. We are causing faith to increase, and we are creating opportunities for angels to work on their behalf.

In the natural, the decrees of a ruling authority are established as law. So it is in the spiritual. When we use our kingly authority to speak forth decrees concerning our young people, we are establishing God's Word as law in their circumstances. Our decrees serve notice to Satan, to the principalities and rulers of darkness, and to all demonic forces that God's Word rules in our lives and in the lives of our young people.

We release our faith through our words, so I urge you to speak and pray audibly when using the strategies. Meditating in your heart is good, but in warfare, the words spoken out of your mouth are far more effective. The Word of God becomes a drawn sword when it comes from a heart in which it has been established (sharpened and polished). And remember, the Word that goes forth from your mouth will not return empty or unproductive. In the authority of Jesus' name it will accomplish what you send it to do.

Finally, I remind you that the material we are about to present is not just for casual reading. You will need to go over it again and again until it is firmly planted in your spirit, heart and mind. Do not forget to insert specific names as much as possible, and to record your Focal Points.

Release your faith now through these strategies to appropriate the promises of God, for His Kingdom to come, and for His will to be done in the lives of our young people.

Please note that most of the prayers, declarations, decrees, and other strategies in Part II are not direct Bible quotations. They personalize and paraphrase the Scriptures referenced.

Chapter Eleven

Strategic Prayers

Prayer is our number one strategy for divine intervention. It is the most powerful tool that God has given humanity to influence matters on the earth. It is also the most powerful weapon we have against Satan's kingdom.

This chapter could simply have been entitled *Prayers,* but we chose *Strategic Prayers* to convey and reinforce certain principles concerning spiritual warfare. In military terms, the word *strategic* refers to that which is "(a) intended to render the enemy incapable of making war, and (b) essential to the conduct of war."[1] It also means "specifically trained or made for destroying enemy bases, industry or communications behind the lines of battle."[2]

You get the picture. We are not dealing with casual prayers. These prayers along with the proclamations, decrees and declarations in subsequent chapters are carefully designed to accomplish the specific purpose of waging war in the heavenlies and bringing about divine intervention. They function like divine projectiles or missiles released in the spirit realm. With divine precision, they hit each target at which they are aimed.

Prayer Perspectives

Persevere in faith. I have heard people ask whether it is a lack of faith to keep on praying about the same thing. The Bible encourages us to persevere and be persistent in prayer, so that is not the problem. What we need to ensure is that we are not using prayer to rehearse our problems before God. Rather, we want to use the privilege of prayer to approach God with a faith-filled heart, make our petitions known to Him, and thank Him for the answer.

Agree for victory. In these prayers I join my faith with yours believing, as the Word of God says, that if two shall agree, being of the same mind and desiring the same thing, it shall be done unto them. We stand in agreement for the full deliverance and restoration of our young people. We agree that we will see them living in victory. (See Matthew 18:19-20.)

Be confident. As you pray, believe in your heart that you will have the things you ask for in prayer.

> Therefore I tell you, whatever you ask for in prayer, believe that you have received it, and it will be yours. (Mark 11:24)

We are praying for restoration in the life of our offspring and other young people, and, by extension, for the future of our nations and God's Kingdom. This is definitely in accordance with God's will, so we can be confident that He will hear and answer our prayers.

> This is the confidence we have in approaching God: that if we ask anything according to his will, he hears us. And if we know that he hears us—whatever we ask—we know that we have what we asked of him. (1 John 5:14-15)

Trust God's timing. Trusting God and the timing in which He chooses to manifest the answer to our prayers is essential. I like this comment from Joel Osteen about trusting God's timing and learning to wait.

> "I would love to tell you that if you prayed hard enough, and if you had enough faith, your prayers would always be answered within twenty-four hours. But that's simply not true. God is not an ATM machine, where you punch in the right codes and receive what you

requested (assuming you've even made a deposit!). No, we all have to wait patiently. That's a part of learning to trust God." [3]

A Few Reminders for Your Engagement in Battle

- Pray offensively. Victory is yours.
- Pray with the authority you have received from Jesus.
- Remain under the covering of God's protective armor, the blood of Jesus and His righteousness.

Now let's take our heavenly position by entering the gates of our God with thanksgiving and His courts with praise.

Prayers of Praise and Thanksgiving

We start off in praise and thanksgiving, and in so doing we lift God to His rightful place of honor above every crisis, every need, and every circumstance. I urge you to wrap all your prayers in praise and thanksgiving, for God inhabits the praises of His people. Our thanksgiving also prepares the way for Him to show us His salvation.

> 11.1 Our Heavenly Father, we take great pleasure in coming to You. We do not take lightly this privilege, so we thank You for it. We enter Your gates with thanksgiving, and Your courts with praise. We give thanks to You and praise You for who You are.
>
> Thank You for the gift of Your Son, Jesus Christ, who gave His life as a ransom for our sins. Thank You for the cross and for His precious blood by which we are forgiven and cleansed. Thank You for the access we have to You, Father, and the boldness we have in coming to You through the blood of Jesus Christ.
>
> We bless You, Lord God of heaven, for there is no God like You. You are holy. You are clothed in majesty and splendor. All power belongs to You. How great You are!

Thank You, Father, for Your unfailing love and tender mercies that endure forever. Your faithfulness continues through all generations. It is more than we can fathom, so we rejoice with grateful hearts and say, Lord, You are good!

We honor You this day as the God of covenant, the God who never fails to keep His promises. For all You have done, Lord, we thank You. And for all that You are going to do, we give You thanks. We choose by faith right now to anchor our hope in You because nothing is too difficult for You. We trust in You, for with You all things are possible.

Bless the Lord, oh my soul, and all that is within me bless His holy name. *Amen.*

Prayers in Honor of God's Name

I love to praise the name of the Lord, for His name expresses His nature and attributes. One of the ways in which God makes Himself known to us is through the many names by which He is called in the Bible.

In the book of Exodus chapter three, God reveals Himself to Moses as the "I AM." That is an unusual name, but here God is telling us that He is self-existent, self-sufficient, and that He is whatever we need.

You may not know all the names of God, but when it comes to praying about the crises in our children's lives, we want to make our appeal to Him using His name that relates to the need. When we do that, we are in essence establishing that attribute and power as supreme over the situation.

Let's honor the name of the Lord through these prayers:

11.2 Oh Lord, our Lord, how excellent is Your name in all the earth. Indeed, Your name is great and greatly to be praised. I lift up the name of Jesus over my offspring, the name that is above every name on the earth and in the heavens. I believe that their knees shall bow to Your strong name, Lord Jesus, and that their tongues shall confess that You are Lord, to the glory and honor of God the Father.

11.3 Lord, in Psalm ninety-one verse fourteen, Your Word says that You will rescue us because You love us, and You will protect us because we acknowledge Your name.

Right now, we acknowledge, bless, and exalt Your holy name. You are the Most High God, the One who is higher than every need and circumstance we face. You are the Almighty God, and besides You there is none other. Great and mighty is Your name. We praise You as our Great Redeemer, Savior, and Mighty Deliverer, who delivers us from the hand of Satan and the power of darkness.

We praise You as Sovereign Lord, for You are the King of kings and Lord of lords. You are our King, our Judge, our Law-giver, and it is You who will save us. You are our Great High Priest who is touched with all our human weaknesses and needs. You are our Healer, the One who heals all our diseases of spirit, soul, and body.

You are our Great Prince of Peace, the One who brings us into wholeness. You are the Lord our Righteousness, our Good Shepherd, who leads us into paths of righteousness for Your name's sake. And thank You for being the God of all Comfort who comforts us in all our trials.

You are the Lord our victory, the One who contends with the enemy on our behalf and gives us the victory again and again. Mighty Conquering Lion of the Tribe of Judah You are; Lord of Heaven's armies who fight on behalf of those who put their trust in You. We praise Your name, O Lord, for all that we need is found in You. *Amen.*

Prayer of Petition to Jesus as Our High Priest

11.4 Jesus, we honor You today as our merciful and faithful High Priest who represents us before God. Thank You for coming to the earth as a human being, just like us, and for dying to take away the sins of humanity. We thank You that You tasted and suffered death for us, and that You broke Satan's power over us and took back the authority he had over us. We acknowledge today that You have done the ultimate. You have done everything to redeem and rescue us. Thank You, Jesus.

We come to You, Great High Priest, on behalf of our young people that have been held captive by the devil. We are asking You to plead their case before the Father so that through the sacrifice of Yourself that You have already offered on their behalf, their sins will be taken away and they will escape from the power of the devil. We ask this in faith believing that as our faithful and merciful High Priest, You are bringing our many sons and daughters into glory. (Hebrews 2:9-17)

Prayer for Taking the Victory Jesus Won for Us

In every battle we need to bear in mind that Jesus has already defeated Satan. As long as we remain in right relationship with God, His victory is ours to claim. In this battle for our young people, we can take by faith what the Word of God tells us that Jesus accomplished on the cross on behalf of all humanity.

11.5 Lord, we thank You that when we were defenseless against the enemy, You defeated him on our behalf and destroyed the power he had over us. You took us out of darkness and brought us into Your wonderful light.

We thank You that as Colossians 2:14-15 tells us, You took away every record of sin that Satan could have used against us. You nailed them to the cross and wiped them out with Your blood. Not only did You do that, but through the cross You disarmed, openly disgraced, and triumphed over Satan and every power of darkness. Thank You for complete victory through Your cross!

And thank You for redeeming us from every curse by taking our curses upon Yourself on the cross. We now declare by faith that we and our young people have been redeemed from every curse and are, by faith, partakers of God's covenant blessings according to Your word in Galatians 3:13-14.

This day we declare that we overcome the enemy by the blood of Jesus and by the word of our testimony. In Jesus' name. *Amen.*

Prayers of Repentance

In our preparation for battle in chapter nine, we repented before God for various shortcomings. But repentance is not only a preparation step. It is a warfare strategy that we practice through prayer. It is not an act that is done once and for all time.

Because the inclination of the fallen human nature is away from, rather than toward God, we need to practice a lifestyle of repentance, which is essentially the sincere turning of our hearts back to God and His ways.

God never shows us all of our sins and shortcomings at once. If He did we wouldn't be able to stand it. His disclosure is an ongoing process that must also be matched by an ongoing process of repentance on our part. So as soon as we become aware of something in our life that displeases God, we ought not to hesitate. We need to repent quickly.

According to Job 22:30, God will deliver the one who is not innocent through the cleanness of another's hands. Clean hands here represent a life cleansed from sin. And Psalm 24:3-4 tells us that it is only those who have clean hands and pure hearts that are able to stand in the presence of the Lord. Praise God for the cleansing power of the blood of Jesus and His gift of righteousness that has been credited to us by faith.

As you can see, a lifestyle of repentance positions us to confidently approach God on behalf of our young people. Here now are some prayer verses of repentance.

11.6 Have mercy on me, O God, according to Your unfailing love; according to Your great compassion blot out my transgressions. Wash away all my iniquity and cleanse me from my sin. For I know my transgressions, and my sin is always before me. Cleanse me with hyssop, and I will be clean; wash me, and I will be whiter than snow. Hide Your face from my sins and blot out all my iniquity. Create in me a clean heart, O God; and renew a right spirit within me. (Psalm 51:1-3, 7, 9-10)

11.7 Search me, O God, and know my heart; test me and know my anxious thoughts. See if there is any offensive way in me, and lead me in the way everlasting. (Psalm 139:23-24)

11.8 Heavenly Father, we have sinned, even as our fathers did; we have done wrong and acted wickedly. (Psalm 106:6)

11.9 O LORD, we acknowledge our wickedness and the guilt of our fathers; we have indeed sinned against You. For the sake of Your name do not despise us; do not dishonor Your glorious throne. Remember Your covenant with us and do not break it. (Jeremiah 14:20-21)

11.10 Father, in the name of Jesus, I ask that You would send in the path of our young people those who would gently instruct them, in the hope that you would grant them repentance leading them to a knowledge of the truth, and that they will come to their senses and escape from the trap of the devil so that he will not hold them captive to do his will. (2 Timothy 2:25-26)

11.11 I pray, in the name of Jesus, that _____ will repent, and turn from all his/her transgressions, so that iniquity will not be his/her ruin. May _____ cast away all transgressions he/she has committed, and receive from You a new heart and a new spirit. (Ezekiel 18:30-31)

Prayer for Forgiveness

11.12 I come on behalf of our young people and ask that You would forgive them for getting involved with the wrong things. In Jesus' name I ask You to forgive their disobedience and rebellion, first to You as their heavenly Father, and also to those You have placed in authority over them. Remove from them the curse for dishonoring their parents and others. I ask for mercy on their behalf, so that they may live long on the earth and so that it may go well with them all the days of their life. Thank You, Father. In Jesus' name. *Amen.*

Prayers for a New Heart

11.13 Heavenly Father, we thank You for Your promise of a new heart. Lord Jesus, You said that whatever we ask of the Father in the authority of Your name, you will do it. So right now, we are asking the same thing that King David asked for: Create in us and in our young people a clean, pure heart, and renew a right spirit within us. Take away the hard, stony, defiled heart and give us a new heart. We ask for hearts that follow after You, Lord, singleness of heart to fear Your name. We praise You right now as the great Surgeon of surgeons, and acknowledge that there is nothing too hard for You. *Amen.*

11.14 By the power of Your grace (Your divine influence), I ask You, Father, to open the hidden places of _____ 's heart, and minister to the deep needs of his/her soul to bring about the change you desire. Pour Your love into _____ 's heart so that he/she will in turn love you with all of his/her heart, soul, and mind. I ask you to give him/her a blameless heart to keep Your commands, Your testimonies and Your laws. I yield myself to you, Lord, as an instrument in the work you desire to do in _____ 's heart. In Jesus' name. *Amen.*

Prayer for Turning the Heart

11.15 Father, you promised in Your Word that You would turn the hearts of children to fathers, and the hearts of fathers to children. We recognize that it is the plan of Satan to deceive us with his lies, to turn our hearts away from you, and destroy our relationships with each other. We repent, Father, for having allowed our hearts to be turned away from You, and ask

You to turn our hearts now; first to You and then to each other: fathers to sons, sons to fathers, mothers to daughters, daughters to mothers, sons to mothers, mothers to sons, daughters to fathers, and fathers to daughters. Reconcile us to each other and heal our relationships, we ask in Jesus' name. *Amen.*

Prayers for Salvation and Deliverance

God desires more than anything else that our young people be saved out of Satan's kingdom of darkness and be set free from every kind of bondage. God, the Father, gave His only begotten Son, Jesus Christ, to die for this very purpose. When we pray for their salvation and deliverance we are touching the very heart of God, and we have the assurance that He will answer our prayers.

11.16 Jesus, I ask You to save and deliver _____ out of every sin and bondage. Only You can do it, Jesus. I trust in You. Jesus saves! Jesus delivers! *Amen.*

11.17 Father, we know it is not Your will that any should perish, but that all should come to repentance. I ask You to give _____ a repentant heart even now. I call _____ an heir of salvation and ask that You would send forth Your ministering spirits to minister to him/her in the way that will cause him/her to turn to You. It is only by Your grace that _____ can be saved and delivered, so I ask You to pour out Your saving grace into his/her heart and cause him/her to respond to You in faith. In Jesus' name. Amen. (2 Peter 3:9, Hebrews 1:14, Ephesians 2:8)

11.18 Father, I ask You to birth a cry for deliverance so deep in _____ 's heart that he/she will cry out to You for help. Thank You, Father, that when our young people cry out in distress You will hear and deliver them. *Amen.*

11.19 I ask you today, Lord, to pour out Your Spirit of grace and supplication upon _____. Cause him/her to look upon You, the One who was pierced and wounded for his/her transgressions.

Cause godly sorrow to arise in _____ 's heart that You might comfort him/her with Your gift of salvation. Amen. (Zechariah 12:10; Isaiah 53:5; 2 Corinthians 7:10; Matthew 5:4)

11.20 Father, in the name of Jesus, I ask You to open the eyes of _____, in order to turn him/her from darkness to light, and from the power of Satan to God, that he/she may receive forgiveness of sins and an inheritance among those who are sanctified by faith. (Acts 26:18)

As scales fell from the eyes of Saul of Tarsus, cause scales to fall from _____ 's eyes. Cause him/her to see Your great light and Your magnificent beauty. Remove the spirit of doubt and unbelief, and give him/her a believing heart to receive Your grace, love, mercy and peace. I believe that by the power of God his/her tongue will confess You as Lord and Savior. In the authority of Jesus' name I pray. *Amen.*

Thank You, Lord, for the promise of deliverance of our offspring and others. According to Your word in Isaiah 49:25, I ask that You would take _____ from the hands of Satan's warriors that have taken him/her captive. And like plunder, retrieve him/her from the hands of the fierce. In Jesus' name we ask You to contend now with the enemy, and save _____ for Your glory. Amen.

Prayers for Divine Intervention

In these prayers we are seeking for God to become actively engaged in the battle for our young people, and for Him to put a restraint on evil.

11.21 We praise You, O Lord, as the mighty, triumphant Warrior. We ask You to arise and scatter the enemies of _____ 's soul. Let his/her foes flee in terror. With one blast of the breath of Your nostrils and with the consuming fire of Your mouth, let every power of darkness that is influencing his/her life be destroyed. (Psalm 68:1; 18:8)

11.22 We realize, Lord, that it is Satan's desire to utterly destroy our young people. But I choose to focus instead on Your superior power over the enemy and Your power to save and deliver _____. All power belongs to You, Great and Mighty God. As You established a boundary for the sea and assigned it to its place, I ask You now, Maker of heaven and earth, to put a restraining order on the spirit of lawlessness that is seeking to overtake _____'s life.

Hold back these secret powers of lawlessness, Lord, and continue to hold them back until they are taken out of the way. Send them now to the places You have reserved for them so they will never again return to harass our lives. This battle is not mine, Lord. It is Yours, and You have never lost a battle.

In the authority of Your name, Jesus, I speak forth this command against the lawless one: 'Enough is enough! Retreat, in Jesus' name. With the blood of Jesus I break Your power over _____'s life and bind up Your works. Your snare is broken and _____'s soul has escaped in Jesus' name.

Now, Lord, I ask You to fulfill your Word. I believe that in your time you will do it swiftly. Amen. (Psalm 62:11; 104:7-9; 2 Thessalonians 2:7; Psalm 124:7; Isaiah 60:22)

Prayers for Divine Protection

Many times, especially as parents, we are tempted to worry when we know or suspect that our young people are going to places and doing things that expose them to danger. I trust that these prayers will help you to focus on God's protective power. You may choose to pray all of them at once or only parts of them at different times.

11.23 Heavenly Father, I thank You that Your will is for our divine protection. Because of Your loving-kindness and Your mercy, we have the privilege of dwelling in the secret place of the Most

High God and abiding under the shadow of the Almighty. Thank You that Your covenant of peace and love with me extends to my offspring, so I am trusting You for their divine protection. (Psalm 91:1-2)

11.24 Be merciful to _____, O Lord and never let him/her go from Your presence. I thank You that there is no place he/she can flee from Your presence. If he/she goes up to the heavens, You are there; if he/she makes his/her bed in the depths, You are there. If he/she rises on the wings of the dawn, if he/she settles on the far side of the sea, even there Your hand will guide him/her, Your right hand will hold him/her securely. If he/she says, "Surely the darkness will hide me and the light will become night around me," I thank You, Lord, that even the darkness will not be dark to You. The night will shine like the day, for darkness is as light to You. (Psalm 139:7-12)

11.25 Although _____ may be going through what seems like the valley of the shadow of death, I will fear no evil, Lord, for I know that You are with him/her and that Your rod and Your staff will comfort (guide, defend, protect, and restrain) him/her. (Psalm 23:4)

11.26 I apply the precious blood of Jesus, our Passover Lamb, upon _____, believing that as the blood protected and pre-served the children of Israel the night that the death angel passed through the land of Egypt, so the blood of Jesus will deliver _____ from the destroyer. (Exodus 12:23)

11.27 Thank You, Lord, that You have given Your angels charge over _____ to accompany, defend and protect him/her in all his/her ways. (Psalm 91:11)

11.28 I ask You to keep _____ as the apple of Your eye. Hide him/her under the shadow of Your wings from the wicked one who would oppress him/her, and from his/her deadly enemies who surround him/her. (Psalm 17:8-9)

11.29 My heart rejoices with thanksgiving, O Lord, for truly You are our rock of defense, our shield, our refuge, and our hiding place. Thank You, Almighty God, and we praise You in Jesus' name. *Amen.*

Prayers for Wholeness

This segment includes prayers for freedom and healing in those areas of the soul that have been used to bring our young people into bondage. These prayers are for the purpose of:

- Shattering strongholds of the mind.
- Healing faulty foundations.
- Gaining freedom from a crisis of identity.
- Bringing about wholeness and peace in general.

11.30 Father, I thank You for the miracle-working power of Your truth and the blood of Jesus to restore and heal the heart and soul. I ask You to forgive _____ for every wrong pattern of thinking, every wrong attitude, habit and belief that has become a stronghold in his/her life. I ask You to free him/her from these strongholds by Your truth and cause every thought to be brought into obedience to Christ.

Tear down, crush, and destroy every barrier to Your healing grace, in Jesus' name. Loose _____ from generational bondages, from strongholds of anger, fear, addictions, rebellion and disobedience, and from any childhood emotional trauma and pain.

Free him/her from the desire for revenge against anyone who has hurt him/her, and give him/her the grace to forgive others even as You have forgiven him/her.

I ask You now to unite _____ 's mind with the mind and thoughts of Christ, and strengthen him/her to walk in the obedience and freedom that are in Christ. In Jesus' name. *Amen.*

11.31 We acknowledge, Father, that out of ignorance the lives of our young people have been built on faulty foundations of ancestral and parental shortcomings and weaknesses. Today we ask for Your forgiveness. Lord, You see the evil infrastructure and the strongholds of deception, unbelief, pride, addiction, rebellion and immorality that the enemy has been building upon these faulty foundations.

In the Name of Jesus I destroy every evil foundation and infrastructure and ask that the consuming fire of heaven would burn and permanently destroy everything of evil in _____ 's heart and life and rebuild him/her in righteousness. Clothe him/her now in Your full armor and Your mighty power so that he/she will resist every temptation of the enemy and flee from evil. Do this for Your glory, Father. In Jesus' name. Amen.

11.32 Father God, You chose to create us as Your image bearers. Thank You that we are so wonderfully and fearfully made. I ask You to forgive us, Father, for having believed the lies of the enemy about who we are.

I pray that _____ will discover Your truth about who he/she really is, and that Your truth will replace all the lies of the enemy. Free him/her from the bondage of negative self-image, low self-worth, and confusion about his/her identity. Help him/her to see himself/herself through Your eyes.

Deliver _____ from the need for the approval of others, from the need to become like others, and from the trap of defining himself/herself by his/her performance, appearance and possessions. Help him/her to esteem the person You created him/her to be. Cause him/her to know, embrace and become secure in Your unconditional love and acceptance.

Renew his/her mind with the truth of Your Word and free him/her to discover and accomplish the purpose for which You created him/her.

11.33 Lord, You are the Great and Mighty Healer. You know all things, and nothing is hidden from You. I ask You to search _____'s heart and look deep into his/her soul and bring healing and wholeness to every wounded and broken place. Pour in Your love and healing oil. You are the God who heals the brokenhearted and binds up their wounds. I ask for Your healing touch upon every emotional wound, and upon any pain of rejection and disappointment. Break through any barriers that _____ might have erected that would block the flow of Your grace and love. Come now, Great Prince of Peace, and fill _____ with Your peace. Instruct him/her in Your peace and restore him/her to complete wholeness. In Jesus' name. Amen   (Psalm 147:3; Luke 4:18; Isaiah 54:3)

11.34 Teach _____ Your way, O Lord, and he/she will walk in Your truth. Unite his/her heart to fear Your name. We will praise You, O Lord our God, with all our hearts, and we will glorify Your name forever. (Psalm 86:11-12)

Prayer to Sever Ungodly Soul Ties

11.35 Lord, Your Word says that bad company corrupts good character. I ask You, Father, to forgive _____ for getting involved with people who have influenced him/her negatively. I ask You now to sever every ungodly soul tie that has been established between _____ and others. Help _____ to come back to his/her senses so that he/she may walk in the ways of good men and keep to the paths of the righteous. You are _____'s provider, Heavenly Father, and I ask You to bless him/her with wise and godly friendships that will help him/her to develop good morals and advance toward the fulfillment of his/her purpose. Thank You for this gift of wholesome relationships for _____. In Jesus' name. Amen. (1 Corinthians 15:33-34; Proverbs 2:20)

Prayer to Break Addictions and Sexual Immorality

11.36 Lord, I come waging war in the Spirit against every manipulating power of darkness that has brought _____ into a state of addiction to habit-forming substances, activities or experiences. *(Specify the name of the addiction if you know what it is.)* In the power and authority of the Name of Jesus that is above every other name, I shatter these strongholds and bind every spirit of addiction and immorality. In the authority You have given me, Jesus, I declare and decree that _____ is now loosed from the influence of every spirit of addiction and immorality, and from the effects of their activities.

I ask, Father, that You now release the healing power of Jesus Christ into _____ 's mind, soul, heart, spirit and body. Destroy every generational inheritance that has created a predisposition to these weaknesses and strengthen him/her by Your grace. Create in _____, I ask You, the desire to fight for his/her own freedom, and bring into his/her path the right kind of help that he/she needs.

Give him/her the power and discipline to resist future temptations, and to avoid relationships and activities that would bring him/her into bondage. Remove his/her appetite for these counterfeit forms of pleasures used to cope with life, and may he/she receive You, Lord Jesus, as the true source of pleasure and every good thing.

I pray that _____ will acknowledge that his/her body belongs to You, and will receive Your grace to present himself/herself as a living sacrifice, holy and acceptable unto You. Thank You that _____ shall no longer yield his/her body as a slave to addictions and immorality, but will yield his/her body to the honor and glory of God. Thank You for setting _____ free, and I enforce this freedom in the mighty Name of Jesus. Amen. (1 Corinthians 6:19; Romans 12:1-2; Romans 6:16)

Prayer for Purpose to Be Revealed

11.37 Heavenly Father, I lift up _____ before You in the mighty name of Jesus. Thank You that You have created _____ for a wonderful purpose. I ask that Your light would shine on his/her path and reveal those things concerning his/her purpose that seem veiled or hidden at this time. Cause the hope of a bright future to spring up on the inside of this dear one, I pray. May he/she see Your good plans that You have for his/her life, and advance steadily towards them without further interference or resistance from the enemy. I claim victory over the enemy on behalf of _____, in the mighty name of Jesus. *Amen.*

Prayer for an Upcoming Court Case

Going through court proceedings that involve a son or daughter is one of the most trying experiences for a parent. This can also be hard on other Hopekeepers who are providing support and encouragement. As you bring your petition to God, I encourage you to believe without a shadow of doubt that even if the outcome is not what you were expecting, it will ultimately be for the best. In these circumstances I remind parents and others that God is extremely economical and wastes nothing. As you pray, believe that God will use this experience as a catalyst for change in the life of the person on trial. Trust in God's ability to work all things for good, and trust in His goodwill toward us that never changes.

11.38 Father, I come in prayer concerning _____ 's upcoming court case. In this matter, Lord, I appeal to the Supreme Court of Heaven, where You preside as _____ 's Judge, Lawgiver, King, and as the One who will save him/her. (Isaiah 33:22)

Great Judge, I come in the Name of Jesus, our Advocate. I come with a plea for mercy. I come pleading the blood of Jesus that was shed and offered to You as payment for _____ 's wrongdoing and transgression. Let the blood prevail, and may

Your mercy triumph over judgment. (James 2:13b)

May Your anger be turned away from _____. Heal his/her backsliding and cause Your love to flow freely to him/her. (Hosea 14:4)

I thank You for Your gracious ruling on _____ 's behalf, and ask that Your will for his/her life that has already been done in heaven be established in the court of the land. Let Your Kingdom come, I pray, and let Your will be done on earth as it is in heaven.

I commit into Your hands every person involved with _____ 's case. I ask that the defense attorney be filled with Your superior wisdom and be blessed with divine favor as he/she represents _____. Move upon the heart of the prosecuting attorney, I pray, and cause Your mercy to flow through him/her. I ask that the judge would submit to Your sovereign authority. May he/she not rule according to what he/she hears or sees in the natural. Instead, let the judge carry out Your judgment and mercy that You have shown to _____.

Now Father, cause _____ to see Your loving-kindness towards him/her, and let the goodness of the Lord lead him/her to repentance. Do not allow one moment of this experience to be wasted, but cause him/her to learn from it. Use it, Father, to turn his/her life around. (Romans 2:4)

I ask that the fear of God would come upon _____ causing him/her to shun the very appearance of evil. Instruct _____ in the way You have chosen for him/her, and cause him/her to willingly follow Your ways. (1 Thessalonians 5:22; Psalm 25:12)

May Your goodness and Your mercy pursue _____ all the days of his/her life, and may he/she dwell in the house of the Lord forever. (Psalm 23:6)

We receive Your verdict, Great Judge, with full assurance that You will work all things for _____ 's good, so that Your purpose for his/her life will come to pass.

I thank You for answering this petition by the power and authority of Jesus' name. *Amen.*

Prayer for Physical Evidence

11.39 Heavenly Father, we ask for the physical manifestation of all that You have accomplished in the spirit realm on behalf of our young people. "Let us, your servants, see your work again; let our children see your glory. And may the Lord our God show us his approval and make our efforts successful. Yes, make our efforts successful!" (Psalm 90:16-17 NLT).

Pray Spontaneously

There are many areas and situations that we have not touched on in these prayers. As you spend time in the Word of God, and learn to listen to the voice of the Holy Spirit, He will lead you in spontaneous prayer concerning the different situations that you will face in this battle. Be bold and courageous and pray as He gives you utterance.

FOCAL POINTS
FOR
STRATEGIC PRAYERS

Record the date and reference number of the prayers that you were impressed to focus on. Be faithful in using them until the Holy Spirit gives you a new focus. Also record any special thoughts that come to mind concerning each Focal Point.

DATE	REFERENCE NUMBER	THOUGHTS AND NOTES

Chapter Twelve

Sending the Word

We are ready now to send or proclaim the Word of God to our offspring and other young people in crisis. You can think of sending the Word as transmitting messages to them via spiritual airwaves. This is a very powerful strategy, especially when we are not in contact with the one for whom we are battling, or when they are not interested in hearing what we have to say. The Word of God is not bound, so we can send it anywhere and anytime. (See 2 Timothy 2:9.)

This strategy of sending the Word is based on two principles: the principle of authority and the principle of precedent. In Luke chapter seven, we read of a centurion who wanted Jesus to heal his servant, but he insisted that there was no need for Jesus to come to his house. He said that Jesus only needed to speak or send the word and his servant would be healed. That is exactly what happened.

Through faith in Jesus we have the same authority in sending the Word. We can also stand on the precedent of Psalm 107:20, which tells us that God sent His Word to those who cried out to Him and He delivered them from their destruction.

We can send the Word with great expectation because God has given us some very sure promises.

1. God promises that His Word will not return empty, void or be unproductive without accomplishing what it was sent to do. (See Isaiah 55:11.)
2. God promises to watch over His Word to perform it—to bring it to pass. (See Jeremiah 1:12.)
3. God promises to carry out the words of His servants. (See Isaiah 44:26.)

One of the names by which God is known is Jehovah Shammah, meaning "The LORD is there" (Ezekiel 48:35). The significance of this name is that God is always present with us. Sending His Word to our young people activates His presence and engages Him in their circumstances. Jesus is the Living Word or the personification of the written Word. Our young people may not be willing to come to Jesus, but He will go to them. When we send the Word we are actually sending Jesus to them.

Our young people may not be willing to come to Jesus, but he will go to them. When we send the Word we are actually sending Jesus to them.

Jesus is the Living Word and He is our hope, so when we send the Word to our young people, we are sending hope to their hearts as an antidote for their despair and spiritual blindness. I find great encouragement in the parable of the lost son in Luke's gospel. (See Luke 15:11-32.) I believe that the father's waiting for his son to return was not a passive kind of waiting. I believe he must have "sent the word" to him, and with that word surrounded him with hope as one strand of the three-fold cord, along with love and faith, that drew him back.

We send the Word because that is how God created us to operate. We are made in His likeness so that we can operate like Him, and God carries out His purposes by speaking. The Bible tells us that He created the universe by the word of His mouth. (See Psalm 33:6; Hebrews 11:3) The word spoken from your mouth in faith is also creative power, for life and death are in the power of your tongue. (See Proverbs 18:21.)

We are going to send the Word in faith because the Bible tells us that the Word of God can be sent, that it produces results, and that it travels with great speed.

- He sent forth His word, and healed them, and delivered them from their destructions. (Psalm 107:20 NKJV)
- He sends His command to the earth; His word runs swiftly. (Psalm 147:15)
- The Lord gives the word [of power]; the women who bear and publish [the news] are a great host. (Psalm 68:11 AMP)
- The entrance of Your words gives light; it gives understanding to the simple. (Psalm 119:130 NKJV)

Psalm 103:20 says that the angels of the Lord obey or harken to the voice of His Word. So begin to see yourself releasing the Word of God from your mouth. See angels being dispatched to bring it to pass. See the one to whom you are sending the Word receiving your sent Word. And see the Word working to produce the purpose for which it is sent.

Are you ready? Let's begin by making a few proclamations to prepare the way for the sent Word.

Listen, O heavens, and I will speak; hear,
O earth, the words of my mouth. (Deuteronomy 32:1)

As the rain and the snow
    come down from heaven,
    and do not return to it
    without watering the earth
    and making it bud and flourish,
    so that it yields seed for the sower and bread for the eater,
so is my word that goes out from my mouth:
    It will not return to me empty,
    but will accomplish what I desire
    and achieve the purpose for which I sent it. (Isaiah 55:10-11)

I speak to every place that has been closed to the Spirit of God:

> Lift up your heads, O you gates;
>> lift them up, you ancient doors,
>> that the King of glory may come in.
> Who is he, this King of glory?
>> The LORD Almighty—
>> he is the King of glory.
> Selah. (Psalm 24:9-10)

First Let There Be Light

Light is necessary for the creation of all that is good, right and true. So the first thing that God did at creation was to call forth light.

Many of our young people are walking in darkness. They cannot even see their true condition. They need the Word of God to be a lamp to their feet and a light for their path. They may have never read the Bible or have stopped reading it, but we can send the light of the Word to them. Jesus is the Light, "the true light that gives light to every man" (John 1:9). Let's send Him to shine on their paths.

12.1　In the authority of Jesus' name, I send the Word of God to you _____, and I say that it shall be a lamp to your feet and a light for your path. I call on Your name, Lord Jesus. You are the Light of the world. I say that even now Your light dispels the darkness in every dark place in _____'s life. Shine, Lord Jesus, shine! For I know that the darkness cannot withstand You. Praise God that _____ is being rescued from Satan's kingdom of darkness and is being transferred even now into Your Kingdom of light. Praise the Lord! Hallelujah! *Amen!* (Psalm 119:105; John 8:12; Colossians 1:13-14)

12.2　_____, I send the Word to you for the light of Jesus Christ to shine in your heart. "For God, who said, 'Let light shine out of darkness,' has made his light shine in your heart to give us the light of the knowledge of the glory of God in the face of Christ" (2 Corinthians 4:6).

12.3 As you receive the light of Jesus Christ, _____, I say to you: Walk in the light! Your day has dawned and the Morning Star arises in your heart. Rise up and follow Him out of darkness into His marvelous light, for you have been delivered from the authority of darkness. (2 Peter 1:19; 1 Peter 2:9; Colossians 1:13-14)

Send the Word to Prepare the Heart

12.4 As the rain of the Word of God falls upon your heart, I say to you, _____, plow up, plow up the hard places of your heart. Break up your fallow ground, the unplowed soil of your heart. Uproot and remove the thorns and thistles. Pull them up at the root. Prepare now for the seed of God's Word to be sown and take root in your heart. No longer shall wickedness be sown in your heart, and no longer shall you reap evil. Today I say to you that you shall sow righteousness and reap unfailing love. (Jeremiah 4:3-4; Hosea 10:12-13)

Send the Word for Repentance

12.5 I send the word of repentance to you, _____. Receive now the grace of God that leads to repentance and a knowledge of the truth. I send the word of 2 Timothy 2:25-26 to you: You will come to your senses and escape from the trap of the devil, who has taken you captive to do his will.

Send the Word for Release from Bondage

12.6 Return now from the land of the enemy. I call you out of the land of oppression and bondage, addictions, immorality, disobedience, rebellion and unbelief. Return to your own land. Return and possess your inheritance of righteousness in Christ

Jesus. I speak to the north, the south, the east and to the west. Give up! You will no longer hold _____ back! Release _____ from your land of wickedness now, in Jesus' name. The Lord calls him/her forth for His glory. Give up and hold not back, in Jesus' name. (Jeremiah 31:17; Isaiah 43:5-7)

12.7 I decree over you, _____, that as the Prodigal Son returned home, even so you shall return to the Lord Jesus Christ. For you were like a sheep going astray, but now you have returned to Jesus, the Shepherd and Overseer of your soul. Even as you turn, the blood of Jesus washes and cleanses you from all unrighteousness. (1 Peter 2:25)

Send the Word of Redemption

12.8 _____, you have been redeemed from the hand of the enemy! Jesus, your Kinsman Redeemer, has paid the full price for your redemption. You are the redeemed of the Lord. You are the righteousness of God, for the Lord has clothed you with garments of salvation, and arrayed you in a robe of righteousness. *Amen.* (Psalm 106:10, 107:2; Isaiah 61:10)

Send the Word of Deliverance, Restoration and Freedom

12.9 I say to you, _____, that as it is written, you shall turn your eyes from worthless things and receive life through the Word of God. (Psalm 119:3)

12.10 In Jesus' name, receive this word of deliverance. _____, you shall not perish, for you shall not believe the lies of the enemy. Neither shall you delight in wickedness or lawlessness, but you shall desire, seek after, love and believe the truth, and so shall you be saved. (2 Thessalonians 2:10-12)

12.11 You will know the truth, and the truth will set you free. The Son sets you free, and you are free indeed. (John 6:32, 36)

12.12 Even now, through Christ Jesus, the law of the Spirit of life is setting you totally free from the law of sin and death. (Romans 8:2)

12.13 Even as God by His command put a limit on the sea and commanded it to go no farther, I send forth the Word of God to restrain the forces of evil in your life. You shall not be consumed by evil. Right now at the sound of my voice the forces of evil are retreating even as the angels of the Lord pursue them and drive them back. As smoke is blown away by the wind, and as wax melts before the fire, so the enemies of your soul shall be blown away and perish. (Psalm 104:7-9; 68:1-2)

12.14 You are the seed of the righteous, _____, and you are delivered from every trap and snare of the enemy. The snare has been broken and you have escaped. I say to you that when the enemy shall come in like a flood, the Spirit of the Lord will lift up a standard against him. Like captives you are taken from warriors. Like plunder you are retrieved from the fierce. The Lord contends with the enemy on your behalf and He saves you from every scheme of the wicked one. (Proverbs 11:21; Psalm 124:7; Isaiah 59:19, 49:25)

12.15 I say to you, _____, that the sun of righteousness has arisen over you with healing, deliverance, and restoration in His wings. You shall go out and leap like a calf released from a stall. You shall trample down the wicked; they shall be ashes under the soles of your feet. Leap! Trample! Know this day that the Lord has done these things on your behalf. (Malachi 4:2-3)

12.16 Break free, _____! The yoke of Satan over your life has been broken by the blood of Jesus. His strongholds are broken! Your spiritual prison doors have swung open! The chains have fallen off! You are free! Free indeed, in Jesus' name! (See Acts 16:26)

Send the Word to Overcome Temptation

12.17 No temptation has taken you, _____, but such as is common to man; but God is faithful. He will not allow you to be tempted beyond what you can bear. And with every temptation He will provide the way of escape so that you will be able to stand up under it.

12.18 I say to you, _____, look and see! The Lord has made a way of escape for you out of this crisis. The Lord is your Shepherd and He will lead you through the valley of the shadow of death into His paths of righteousness. Take the way of the Lord; it is your way of escape. Humble yourself. Do not be stubborn. You cannot save yourself. Your salvation comes from the Lord. Put your trust in Him!

Send the Word for Godly Relationships

12.19 In the name of the Lord Jesus Christ I send the Word to you, _____, that is able to pull down all ungodly relationships and corrupting influences that have been promoted in your life by the kingdom of darkness. By the power of the living and sharp Word of God, you are being separated right now from every unwholesome soul-tie. The blood of Jesus establishes a filter between you and such influences even now. I say to you that your life shall now attract only wholesome friendships and relationships for the glory of God. *Amen.*

12.20 I call you blessed this day, for you shall no longer walk in the counsel of the ungodly, or stand in the way of sinners, or sit in the seat of mockers. You will delight in the law of the Lord, walking in the ways of good men and keeping to the paths of the righteous. Surely goodness and mercy shall follow you all the days of your life and you shall dwell in the house of the Lord forever. (Psalm 1:1-2; Proverbs 2:20; Psalm 23:6)

Send the Word of Peace

12.21 You shall be taught of the Lord, the God of Peace. He shall be your Jehovah Shalom, and great shall be your peace. In righteousness you shall be established. (Isaiah 54:13-14a)

12.22 As Jesus has said, I say to you, _____, "Peace I leave with you;

my peace I give you. I do not give to you as the world gives" (John 14:27).

12.23 Receive now the peace of Jesus Christ, the peace that is beyond human understanding. Receive the wholeness and prosperity that Jesus gives, and there shall be nothing missing and nothing broken in your life.

Send the Word for Healing and Wholeness

12.24 Psalm 107:17-20 says the Lord sent His Word and healed those who had become fools through their rebellious ways and who suffered affliction because of their iniquities. They cried to the Lord in their trouble, and He saved them. Even now, _____, I call forth such a cry from your heart and from your mouth. Cry out to the Lord God Almighty, your strong deliverer, for it is He who will save you. In the authority of the strong name of Jesus I now send the word of healing to the deepest recesses of your soul. Be healed of every kind of disease that has afflicted your soul. May your soul prosper in Jesus' name.

Send the Word to Become Anchored in God's Love

12.25 _____, I send the Word of your heavenly Father's unfailing love to you. You will know, understand, recognize, be conscious of, believe, and receive the love that God your Father has for you. Nothing in all creation can separate you from the love of your heavenly Father. You are His beloved child. Be established now in His perfect love that drives out all fear from your heart. (1 John 4:16, 18)

Send the Word of Hope

12.26 Now, _____, the God of hope fill you with all joy and peace in believing. And I say to you, be filled with hope by the power of the Holy Spirit. There is hope for your future, for every one of God's good plans for your life will come to pass. (Romans 15:13; Jeremiah 29:11)

12.27 Hope deferred makes the heart sick, but I say to you, _____, that your hope shall no longer be deferred. You will see your dreams come true and you will be filled with life and joy. (Proverbs 13:12)

Send the Word for God's Blessing and the Outpouring of His Spirit

12.28 The Spirit of the Lord is being poured out upon you, _____, and His blessing is working in you, on you, and around you. You shall spring up like grass in a meadow and like poplar trees by flowing streams. You shall prosper like a tree planted by streams of water which yields its fruit in season and whose leaf does not wither. (Isaiah 44:4; Psalm 1:3)

Prayer of Thanksgiving to Seal the Sent Word

Father, I thank You for the authority You have given me to send Your Word. Thank You that Your Word that I have released over _____'s life and sent to his/her heart has within it the power to fulfill itself. I thank You that not one of Your words that I have spoken shall fall to the ground. I thank You that they shall not return void, empty or use-less, without producing any effect, but they shall accomplish every-thing for which they have been sent. Thank You for Your angels who respond to Your Word. They have heard the Word that I have spoken and I believe that they are going about to bring every Word to pass. I thank You for the precious blood of Jesus, and I apply it now as a seal upon every sent Word. Thank You for the life that is in the blood which is even now preserving, giving life to, and activating every Word to produce what it is sent to do. In Jesus' name. Amen.

FOCAL POINTS
FOR
SENDING THE WORD

Record the date and reference number of the proclamations that you were impressed to focus on. Be faithful in using them until the Holy Spirit gives you a new focus. Also record any special thoughts that come to mind concerning each Focal Point.

DATE	REFERENCE NUMBER	THOUGHTS AND NOTES

Chapter Thirteen

Declarations and Decrees

I n the prayer strategy you prayed God's Word back to Him. In sending the Word, you sent telegraphic messages from the Word of God to the spirits and hearts of those in crisis. Now, in your declarations and decrees you will be using a different strategy.

1. You are speaking forth God's will, plan, and purpose, and making it known to the spiritual forces of darkness against which we wrestle. (See Ephesians 3:10, 6:12.)
2. You are making God's will, plan, and purpose law on the earth as it has already been established in heaven. (See Psalm 119:89; Matthew 6:10.)
3. You are giving voice to the law of God so that He can command His angels to enforce it. (See Psalm 103:20-21.)

While you function in your priestly authority in prayer, in making declarations and decrees, you are exercising both your prophetic and kingly authority. This is the exercise of the dominion authority to rule the earth that was given to humanity at creation, was lost through Adam, and was restored through Jesus Christ.

The dictionary defines decree as "a decision or order made by one in authority; something ordered or established by law." As believers in Christ we stand in a place of authority over all the power of the enemy. This includes having the authority to legislate, in the spiritual realm, God's will, plan, and purposes into the lives of our young people. (See Matthew 10:1, 16:19; Luke 10:19.)

We understand from Colossians 2:14-15 and Galatians 3:13-14 that Jesus took away and nailed to the cross every record of our transgressions, every curse, and every evil decree that was against us. By faith in Jesus' complete work of redemption on the cross, we can establish new decrees to appropriate what has already been accomplished.

Remember, when you are speaking in the authority of Jesus Christ, you have the force or power of the Almighty, the Most High God, behind the words you speak.

The declarations and decrees in this chapter are examples of "new laws" based on the Word of God that you will use to cancel and supersede every evil order of the enemy concerning our young people's lives. According to Psalm 45:1, your tongue is the "pen of a ready writer." By speaking forth these declarations and decrees, you are actually writing and establishing God's law and government in the life of the one on whose behalf you are speaking. You are superimposing God's prophetic purposes for their lives over the assignments of the enemy.

This is what the Scripture says about your authority:

- Thou shalt also decree a thing, and it shall be established unto thee. (Job 22:28 KJV)
- Behold! I have given you authority and power to trample upon serpents and scorpions, and [physical and mental strength and ability] over all the power that the enemy [possesses]; and nothing shall in any way harm you. (Luke 10:19 AMP)

Remember, when you are speaking in the authority of Jesus Christ, you have the force or power of the Almighty, the Most High God, behind the words you speak. When God sent Moses to Pharaoh with His Word, He said that Moses would be like God to Pharaoh. So it is for us. When we are in right standing with God and speak in His authority, God's power backs our word and it is as if God Himself were speaking.

You will also need to develop your God-given power of visualization as you speak forth your declarations and decrees. Train yourself to see and to hold in your mind images of the desired end result. These are your hope pictures. And do not allow yourself to become discouraged if what you are presently seeing in the natural does not line up with your declarations and decrees or with your hope images. Persevere in faith. Continue to do what God does—keep calling things that are not as though they were. That is to say, continue speaking of things not as they are presently but as you desire them to become. (See Romans 4:17.)

In speaking forth declarations and decrees, you stand on the same sure promises as when you are sending the Word.

1. God promises that His Word will not return empty, void or be unproductive without accomplishing what it was sent to do. (See Isaiah 55:11.)
3. God promises to watch over His Word to perform it—to bring it to pass. (See Jeremiah 1:12.)
4. God promises to carry out the words of His servants. (See Isaiah 44:26.)

Let's now speak forth our proclamations to prepare the way for the declarations and decrees we are about to establish.

Listen, O heavens, and I will speak; hear, O earth, the words of my mouth. (Deuteronomy 32:1)

For the LORD of hosts hath purposed, and who shall disannul it? and his hand is stretched out and who shall turn it back? (Isaiah 14:27 KJV)

As the rain and the snow
  come down from heaven,

and do not return to it
without watering the earth
and making it bud and flourish,
so that it yields seed for the sower and bread for the eater,
so is my word that goes out from my mouth:
It will not return to me empty,
but will accomplish what I desire
and achieve the purpose for which I sent it. (Isaiah 55:10-11)

As you speak, stand on the authority of Job 22:28, you shall decree a thing and it shall come to pass. Do you want to see your young people established in righteousness? Then decree it!

Decree Against Satan's Judgments

13.1　On the authority that Jesus has given me over all the power of the devil, I decree that all destructive judgments and resolutions against our young people are transformed this day into divine decrees of great deliverance, mercy, love and peace. *Amen.*

Decree to Bind the Strongman

13.2　On the authority of Jesus' name, I decree that every strongman over _____'s life is bound. _____ is now loosed from the hold of every strongman. Their authority and power over his/her life is terminated, and _____ is free from their reign of terror. In Jesus' name. *Amen.* (Matthew 12:29)

Decree Terminating Assignments of Evil

13.3　Jesus has given me authority over all the power of the enemy, and in that authority I decree that every evil assignment against _____'s life is terminated. As Elijah, a man of faith, called for consuming fire from heaven, so now I decree that this same covenant-keeping God consumes the practitioners of evil and their wicked assignments to destroy _____. God's Word in my mouth is as fire, and with one blast of the breath of the Almighty they are consumed. I decree that every evil power that rages against _____ will surely be ashamed and disgraced. (1 Kings 18:22-38; 2 Kings 1:10, 12)

Decree Against the Advance of Evil

13.4   As God the Creator, Sovereign Ruler and Judge, put a limit on the sea and commanded it to go no further, even now, I decree a divine restraint on the spirit of lawlessness that has been at work in _____s life. I decree, by the authority of Jesus Christ, that the progression of evil in _____'s life is now arrested. I decree that he/she belongs to the Lord, and shall serve the Lord. _____ is God's property. _____'s life is no longer a thoroughfare for evil, satanic invasion, trespass, or occupation. I put the blood of Jesus and the power of the cross as a filter between _____'s life and every force of darkness. In Jesus' mighty name. *Amen.* (2 Thessalonians 2:7; Joshua 24:15; Revelation 12:11)

Declarations of Deliverance

13.5   As God anointed Jesus of Nazareth and He went about doing good, healing and delivering all who were oppressed of the devil, I declare that the Spirit of the Sovereign LORD is also upon me to proclaim the deliverance of our young people from bondage. He has anointed me to proclaim freedom for the captives and release from darkness for the prisoners. (Acts 10:38; Isaiah 61:1)

13.6   Though the wicked join forces, I declare that they shall not go unpunished, but the seed of the righteous will be delivered. (Proverbs 11:21)

13.7   I declare that the Sovereign Lord, the Lord of Hosts, has set His face against every evil practitioner that has ensnared _____'s soul. The Sovereign Lord has rescued _____ from the hand of every evil practitioner, and from the lies that they have used to make his/her heart sad, discouraged and rebellious. By the power of the blood of Jesus, the hold of Satan over _____'s life is broken._____ is delivered out of Satan's kingdom of darkness and is transferred into the Kingdom of God's dear Son. (Ezekiel 13:20-23; Colossians 1:13)

13.8 You ask, "can plunder be taken from warriors, / or captives rescued from the fierce? / But this is what the LORD says: / 'Yes, captives will be taken from warriors, and plunder retrieved from the fierce; / I will contend with those who contend with you, / and your children I will save'" (Isaiah 49:25).

13.9 The Lord shall deliver _____ from every evil attack and preserve him/her for His heavenly Kingdom. (2 Timothy 4:18)

13.10 The god of this world will no longer blind _____'s mind to the truth. By the authority and power of the name of Jesus, I break Satan's power over his/her life. I claim _____'s deliverance in Jesus' name. (2 Corinthians 4:3-4)

Declaration against Enemy Strongholds of the Mind

13.11 I declare in the authority of the name of Jesus that _____ has the mind of Christ. Every enemy stronghold in his/her mind is now being destroyed by the power of Jesus' name. Every thought and every attitude that would exalt itself above the knowledge of God is now taken captive and brought into obedience to the will and purposes of God. (2 Corinthians 10:3-6)

Decree of Order

13.12 I decree order in _____'s life. Let there be light. Let order come forth out of chaos. Let God's creative work be accomplished in his/her life now! *Amen.* (Genesis 1:3)

Declarations for Repentance and Salvation

13.13 I declare by faith that _____ shall come to repentance and the saving knowledge of the truth. His/her knees shall bow to the authority of Jesus Christ, and his/her mouth shall confess that Jesus Christ is Lord. (Romans 10:9-10; 2 Timothy 2:26)

13.14 I declare that _____ is one who through faith is being shielded by God's power until the coming of the salvation that is ready to be revealed in him/her by the grace of God. (1 Peter 1:5)

13.15 I declare that _____ has been appointed for eternal life. He/she shall believe the Good News of the Gospel in Jesus Christ and shall be saved. (Acts 13:48)

13.16 I am a believer in the Lord Jesus Christ, therefore, I declare that _____ and all of my descendants are saved. As for me and my house, we shall serve the Lord. (Acts 16:31; Joshua 24:15)

Decrees of Freedom

13.17 In the name of Jesus, I decree that the power of Almighty God breaks the hold of every captive and every warrior over _____'s life. Their grip is loosened and their influence is nullified. I decree that _____ is rescued and set free by the saving power of the Lord Jesus Christ. (Isaiah 49:25)

13.18 In due season _____ shall be liberated from bondage and brought into the glorious freedom of the children of God. (Romans 8:21)

13.19 In the name of Jesus, I decree that _____ shall know the truth, believe the truth, and continue in the truth. The truth shall set him/her free. I decree that because the Son sets _____ free, he/she is free indeed! (John 8:32, 36)

Decrees and Declarations of Victory

13.20 I decree that no weapon of the enemy formed against _____ shall prosper, and I condemn every judgment of the enemy against his/her life in Jesus' name. (Isaiah 54:17)

13.21 I decree that _____ shall possess the gates of his/her enemy and shall have victory over every satanic force that has risen up against him/her to control his/her mind and heart. (Genesis 22:17)

13.22 I decree that everything meant for evil in _____'s life shall be turned to good. He/she is more than a conqueror through Christ Jesus who loved him/her and gave His life for him/her. (Romans 8:28, 37)

13.23 I declare that our Redeemer is strong; the Lord Almighty is His name: He shall thoroughly plead _____'s cause, that He may give rest to him/her and disquiet the enemy of his/her soul. (Jeremiah 50:34)

13.24 As birds flying, so will the LORD of Hosts defend _____; defending also He will deliver him/her; and passing over, He will preserve him/her. (Isaiah 31:5)

Declarations of Family Blessing

13.25 I declare that through the sacrifice of Jesus Christ on the cross that completely atoned for our sin and accomplished our full redemption, I and my offspring have been redeemed from every curse of every sin and have entered into the blessing of Abraham, whom God blessed in all things. (Galatians 3:13; Genesis 12:2-3)

13.26 I declare that instead of shame I and my offspring will receive a double portion of blessing and honor, and instead of disgrace, we will rejoice in our inheritance of righteousness that is from the Lord. We will inherit our double portion blessing, and everlasting joy will be ours. For the LORD loves justice; He hates robbery and iniquity. In His faithfulness He will reward us and make an everlasting covenant with us. My descendants be known among the nations, and my offspring among the peoples. All who see us will acknowledge that we are a people the LORD has blessed. (Isaiah 61:7-9)

13.27 I have not toiled in vain or borne children doomed to misfortune. I am blessed by the LORD, I and my descendants with me. (Isaiah 65:23)

13.28 I decree that my offspring will live in the presence of the Lord and their descendants will be established before Him. I am the servant of the Lord, and this promise is mine in Jesus' name. (Psalm 102:28)

13.29 My seed shall continue after me and be established before God. They shall be mighty upon the earth. (Psalm 102:28, 112:2)

13.30 I declare the Word of the Lord that though the mountains be shaken and the hills be removed, His unfailing love for me and my offspring will not be shaken, neither shall His covenant of peace with us be removed. (Isaiah 54:10)

Declarations of Hope and Peace

13.31 I declare that there is hope for _____'s future, for he/she shall return from the land of the enemy. I declare that every one of God's good plans for his/her life will come to pass, and that I shall see the goodness of the Lord manifested in his/her life while I am still in the land of the living. (Jeremiah 31:17, 29:11; Psalm 27:13)

13.32 I declare that _____ is taught of the Lord and great is his/her peace, and that he/she shall be established in righteousness. (Isaiah 54:13-14)

Sealing Your Decrees and Declarations

Every decree and declaration that I have spoken out of my mouth is written and sealed by the authority of Jesus Christ and His precious blood. They cancel, nullify and supersede every evil decree and declaration that had previously governed the life of our young people. I decree it to be so, and the Lord God Almighty confirms it to be so. Amen.

FOCAL POINTS
FOR
DECLARATIONS AND DECREES

Record the date and reference number of the declarations and decrees that you were impressed to focus on. Be faithful in using them until the Holy Spirit gives you a new focus. Also record any special thoughts that come to mind concerning each Focal Point.

DATE	REFERENCE NUMBER	THOUGHTS AND NOTES

Chapter Fourteen

Personal Daily Faith Confessions

The emphasis of the previous three strategies has been on how to fight on behalf of our young people in crisis. But as a Hopekeeper you are likely to face the same peril as that of a caregiver. You are likely to give out more than you take in. You are likely to overlook your personal need for reinforcement, and before you know it your faith and your hope may start slipping.

This strategy is first of all for your personal benefit. Ultimately others will benefit, for you will be better equipped for the battle when your hope, your faith, and your inner strength are restored. This strategy requires you to daily speak aloud confession of faith from God's Word.

Your daily faith confessions serve at least four purposes:

1. To reinforce your hope by constantly reminding you of the hope that is in you.
2. To build, release and exercise your faith. Faith comes from hearing the Word of God.
3. To keep you in the creative mode. As someone has said, if you're not speaking, you're not creating.
4. To encourage yourself in the Lord. That is what the Bible tells us that King David did when he was faced with overwhelming trials and circumstances.

We encourage you to include some or all of these hope scriptures in your daily faith confessions.

14.1 I confess that right now as I release my faith to believe, the God of hope is filling me with all joy and peace so that by the power of His Holy Spirit I may abound and be overflowing, bubbling over with hope. (Romans 15:13)

14.2 I choose to be of good cheer because Jesus has overcome the world, including every trial and circumstance I am facing. He has deprived it of power to harm me. I am confident of this and undaunted by what I see, hear and feel. (John 16:33 AMP)

14.3 Through my steadfast and patient endurance, and through the encouragement of the Scriptures, I boldly confess that I have hope. (Romans 15:4)

14.4 I will not allow my soul to be disquieted, downcast or disturbed with worry, fear or unbelief. I make a demand on my soul to hope in God. My soul, put your hope in God, for I will praise Him, my Savior and my God. (Psalm 42:5, 11)

14.5 As for me, I will always have hope. I will praise the Lord more and more. (Psalm 71:14)

14.6 My soul, wait patiently for God alone, for my expectation is from Him. He only is my rock and my salvation; He is my defense; I shall not be moved. In God is my salvation and my glory: the rock of my strength. My refuge is in God. (Psalm 62:5-7)

14.7 My help is in the name of the Lord, the Maker of heaven and earth. So I take comfort and I am encouraged, and say with confidence and boldness: 'The Lord is my Helper; I will not be seized with alarm. I will not fear or dread or be terrified.' (Psalm 124:8; Hebrews 13:6 AMP)

14.8 God is my refuge and strength, an ever-present help in trouble. Therefore, I will not fear. When I am afraid I will trust in God. I will trust in God, whose Word I praise. I will not be afraid. (Psalm 46:1-2a, 56:3-4)

14.9 I will have no fear of bad news; my heart is steadfast, trusting in the LORD. My heart is secure, I will have no fear; in the end I will look in triumph on my foes. (Psalm 112:7-8)

14.10 As for me, I watch in hope for the Lord; I wait for God my Savior; my God will hear me. (Micah 7:7)

14.11 Some trust in chariots and some in horses, but I trust in the name of the Lord. (Psalm 20:7)

14.12 I rejoice in the strength of the Lord. Great are the victories He has given me. He has granted me the desire of my heart and has not withheld the request of my lips. (Psalm 21:1-2)

14.13 The Lord is my Strength and my impenetrable Shield; my heart trusts in, relies on, and confidently leans on Him, and I am helped; therefore my heart greatly rejoices, and with my song will I praise Him. (Psalm 28:7 AMP)

14.14 I am a believer, not a doubter. I have a believing heart. I will not lose heart, because I believe that I will see the goodness of the Lord in the land of the living. I will wait on the Lord. I will be strong and courageous, for He will strengthen my heart. (Psalm 27:13-14)

14.15 I will set a guard over my mouth and keep watch over the door of my lips. I will speak only what is good and beneficial that it may impart grace and strength. (Psalm 141:3; Ephesians 4:29)

14.16 Though I may not yet see the manifestation of what I am believing for, yet I will rejoice in the Lord. I will joy in the God of my salvation. (Habakkuk 3:17-18)

14.17 Against my human reasoning, I will continue believing in hope. I will not be weakened in faith or waver through unbelief regarding the promises of God. I will be strengthened in faith and give glory to God, for I am fully persuaded that God has all power to do what He has promised. (Romans 4:18-21)

14.18 I live by faith and not by sight. Therefore, I will not be moved by what I see or what I hear. I trust in God who gives life to the dead, and like Him, I call things that are not as though they were already manifested. (2 Corinthians 5:7; Romans 4:17)

14.19 I lean on, trust in, and am confident in the Lord with all my heart and mind, and I do not rely on my own insight or understanding. In all my ways I know, recognize, and acknowledge Him, and He directs and makes straight and plain my paths. I am not wise in my own eyes, but I reverently fear and worship the Lord and turn entirely away from evil. This shall be health to my nerves and sinews, and marrow and moistening to my bones. (Proverbs 3:5-8 AMP)

14.20 I have the wisdom of God, for the Spirit of Truth abides in me and teaches me all things. Therefore, I know what to do in every situation that I come up against. (John 14:17; 16:13)

14.21 I will not throw away my confidence, for I know it will be richly rewarded. I will persevere, knowing that when I have done the will of God I will receive what He has promised. (Hebrews 10:35-36)

14.22 I hold unswervingly and without wavering to the hope and faith that I profess, knowing that God is reliable, sure, and faithful to fulfill every one of His promises. (Hebrews 10:23)

14.23 I have set the LORD always before me; because He is at my right hand I shall not be moved. Therefore my heart is glad, and my glory rejoices; my flesh also will rest in hope. (Psalm 16:8-9 NKJV)

14.24 I put my trust in the Lord, who is my rock and my refuge. I will never be disappointed or put to shame. (Psalm 25:2, 20; 31:1, 3)

14.25 I clothe myself in the full armor of God. I am therefore able to successfully stand against all the strategies and deceit of the devil. (Ephesians 6:11 AMP)

14.26 I am hard pressed on every side, but not crushed; perplexed, but not in despair; persecuted, but not abandoned; struck down, but not destroyed. Therefore I do not lose heart. I fix my eyes not on what is seen, but on what is unseen, for what is seen is temporary, but what is unseen is eternal. (2 Corinthians 4:8, 16a, 18)

14.27 Yet I still dare to hope when I remember this: The faithful love of the LORD never ends! His mercies never cease. Great is His faithfulness; His mercies begin afresh each morning. (Lamentations 3:21-23)

14.28 There is surely a future hope and reward for me; there is an end, and my expectation and hope will not be cut off. (Proverbs 23:18)

14.29 I am counting on the Lord. Yes, I am counting on Him. I have put my hope in His Word. (Psalm 130:5 NLT)

When the circumstances in the life of the one for whom you are doing battle fly in the face of your hope, when what you see and what you hear defy your faith, anchor yourself in the Most High God who is mighty to save.

14.30 I refuse to worry about anything. I cast all my cares for _____'s life on the Lord because He cares for us. (1 Peter 5:7)

14.31 I am not moved by what I see or hear concerning _____. I trust in the power of the sovereign Lord who causes all things to work for the good of those who love Him. I love you, Lord, and I believe that you will deliver _____ from every deadly peril. I set my hope on you, Lord God Almighty, that you have delivered _____ and that you will continue delivering him/her. (Romans 8:28; 2 Corinthians 1:10)

14.32 I believe that God is able to do immeasurably more than all I could ask or imagine in _____'s life. (Ephesians 3:20)

14.33 I commit my way to the Lord, I trust also in Him and He will bring to pass His will for _____'s deliverance. (Psalm 37:5)

14.34 No weapon that is formed against _____'s life will prosper, and every tongue that rises in judgment against him/her I refute, for this is my heritage as a servant of the Lord. (Isaiah 54:17)

14.35 I wait for the Lord, my soul waits, and in His word I put my hope. My soul waits for the Lord more than watchmen wait for the morning. I put my hope in the Lord, for with the Lord is unfailing love and with Him is full redemption. He Himself has redeemed _____ from all his/her sins. (Psalm 130:5-8)

14.36 The Lord will perfect that which concerns me. He has started a good work in _____'s life, and I am confident that He will finish it. (Psalm 138:8; Philippians 1:6)

14.37 *I* am filled with hope for _____'s future. By faith, I see every one of God's good plans for his/her life coming to pass. I confess that I have this anchor of my soul, both firm and secure. I shall not be moved. (Jeremiah 29:11; Hebrews 6:19)

14.38 I will not grow weary in doing good and in keeping hope alive for _____'s deliverance, for in due season I know that I will reap if I faint not. (Galatians 6:9)

14.39 The Lord is faithful. He will strengthen and protect _____ from the evil one. (2 Thessalonians 3:3)

These next seven confessions are specific to Hopekeeper parents and their offspring.

14.40 I am the servant of the Lord; therefore I confess that my offspring will live in the presence of the Lord, and their descendants will be established before Him. (Psalm 102:28)

14.41 I choose this day that as for me and my offspring we will serve the Lord. (Joshua 24:15)

14.42 The blood of Jesus is upon me, upon my household, and upon all my offspring, therefore the wicked one cannot destroy us. I believe in the Lord Jesus Christ and I am saved. As the Word of God promises, I declare that my entire household and all of my offspring are saved as well. (Exodus 12:13; Acts 16:31)

14.43 I have not toiled in vain or borne children doomed to misfortune. I am blessed of the Lord, I and my descendants with me. (Isaiah 65:23)

14.44 I proclaim that the Lord Almighty has fortified the bars of my gates and blessed my children within my gates. (Psalm 147:13 NLT)

14.45 God's covenant is with me and His Spirit is on me. His words that He has put in my mouth will not depart from my mouth, or the mouths of my children, or from the mouths of their descendants from this time on and forever. (Isaiah 59:21)

14.46 I refrain my voice from weeping and my eyes from tears, for my work will be rewarded as the Lord has declared. My children will return from the land of the enemy. There is hope for my future and the future of my offspring, for they will return to the Lord. (Jeremiah 31:16-17)

As with the other strategies, we encourage you to find other Bible-based confessions and add them to this compilation.

Stay in faith and keep your hope alive!

FOCAL POINTS
FOR
PERSONAL DAILY FAITH CONFESSIONS

Record the date and reference number of the daily faith confessions that you were impressed to focus on. Be faithful in using them until the Holy Spirit gives you a new focus. Also record any special thoughts that come to mind concerning each Focal Point.

DATE	REFERENCE NUMBER	THOUGHTS AND NOTES

Chapter Fifteen

Supplementary Strategies

So far we have presented four essential strategies for keeping hope alive in the battle for our grown children and other young people in crisis: praying strategic prayers; sending the word; making declarations and decrees; and speaking daily faith confessions.

In this chapter we will be covering a total of eight supplementary strategies that will help you do battle on a whole new level for the breakthrough you so desire.

Supplementary Strategy #1: Join Forces with Others

If you are a parent whose teenager or young adult is in crisis, be aware that Satan will try to use the weapons of shame and isolation against you. It is natural to feel some embarrassment about the lifestyle that our offspring are leading or the trouble they have fallen into. But the enemy takes advantage of these feelings and moves in with the suggestion that we had better keep it a secret to save ourselves from further shame. It is a deadly trap, however, and we will fall for it if we try to fight the battle on our own.

While it would be unwise to rehearse or unnecessarily expose the details of their crises, there is much advantage to be gained from joining forces with others. As was mentioned in chapter eight, we will also increase our power base when men and fathers take their place with women and mothers in the battle and join forces as God's team of Hopekeeper warriors.

There is power in agreement:

> Again I say unto you, that if two of you shall agree on earth as touching any thing that they shall ask, it shall be done for them of my Father which is in heaven. (Matthew 18:19 KJV)

The Amplified Bible translation of that verse helps us to understand that agreeing means to "harmonize together, make a symphony together."

When we pray with other Hopekeepers, it is important to ensure that we are one with the will of God for that particular situation. I stress this because unless we wait on the Holy Spirit to reveal the mind of God in a matter, it is easy to pray according to our preconceptions and even the suggestions of the enemy.

Waiting before God is essential in warfare. It is the process by which we receive instruction from our Commander in Chief, and unite ourselves as one with Him in battle.

There is strength and multiplied victory in numbers:

> Five of you shall chase a hundred, and a hundred of you shall put ten thousand to flight; your enemies shall fall by the sword before you. (Leviticus 26:8 NKJV)

> One can chase a thousand, but two can put ten thousand to flight. (Adapted from Deuteronomy 32:30)

> Two are better than one,
>   because they have a good return for their work:
> If one falls down,
>   his friend can help him up.
>   But pity the man who falls
>   and has no one to help him up!
> Though one may be overpowered,

two can defend themselves.
A cord of three strands is not quickly broken.
(Ecclesiastes 4: 9-10, 12)

There is safety in the wise counsel of others:

Where no wise guidance is, the people fall, but in the multitude of counselors there is safety. (Proverbs 11:14 AMP)

God will use others and the wisdom they have gained through their own painful experiences to guide you through your present crisis. By meeting with others for prayer, fellowship and instruction, you will be able to tap into the anointing that is on their lives and thereby enlarge your capacity for the battle. You will even gain insight into the strategies for fighting your particular battle as you gather with others in one accord and wait in the presence of the Lord for His Word. Comfort, encouragement, strength, and hope will also flow to you through this kind of fellowship.

So we encourage you to connect with other Hopekeepers. It does not even have to be someone with similar experiences. There are many believers who are strong in faith and have a burden to see young people delivered out of bondage. Whatever you do, do not fall for the enemy's trap of isolation. Join your faith with others in a prayer network. And do not hesitate to organize a group if necessary. You will be amazed at the results.

Supplementary Strategy #2: Make a Plea in Heaven's Court

You may recall from an earlier chapter that we said the spiritual battle in which we are engaged for our young people also has legal dimensions. Although God is not legalistic, He establishes and adheres to laws and covenants. When we know the principles by which God operates and we are living by them, we have the opportunity of going before Him on behalf of our young people with a plea based on the legal principles of His Kingdom.

God actually invites us to present and plead our cases with Him.

Put Me in remembrance [remind Me of your merits]; let us plead and argue together. Set forth your case, that you may be justified (proved right). (Isaiah 43:26 AMP)

No one calls for justice; no one pleads his case with integrity. They rely on empty arguments and speak lies; they conceive trouble and give birth to evil. (Isaiah 59:4)

The challenge many of us face is that we are not familiar with these kinds of proceedings either in the natural or in the spiritual. A full review of this process is outside the scope of this book. However, to further explore the subject of pleading the case of others in prayer, I encourage you to read the book, *The Advocates,* by Eddie and Alice Smith. To help you get started, we have provided you with a few key points below, and a sample plea for grace and mercy.

1. Approach God as the Sovereign Judge of the highest court in heaven and earth. One of the names of God in the Bible is Sovereign LORD. Not only is He the Supreme Ruler. He is the most powerful One, who has power over the **outcome** of all things. (This is different from controlling all things which would require taking away an individual's free will and power of choice.) Ascribe to God even greater honor than you would to a judge of the land. Address Him as Supreme and Sovereign Judge. "For the LORD is our judge, / the LORD is our lawgiver, / the LORD is our king; / it is he who will save us." (Isaiah 33:22)

2. See yourself as an advocate. You are representing others on earth, but Jesus will represent you and them in the courts of heaven. The stronger your relationship is with this Advocate and with the Judge, the more effective your plea will be.

3. Plead with integrity. Speak truth by relying on God's Word. Many of the Scriptures used in the prayers and declarations in

earlier chapters can also be used for this purpose. Approach God with a heart of true repentance. As Job 22:30 says, "He will deliver even one who is not innocent, / who will be delivered through the cleanness of your hands."

4. Put your faith in Jesus' work of redemption. What Jesus has accomplished on behalf of all humanity is the principal ground on which you make each plea. Jesus took every curse for our disobedience upon Himself and nailed them to the cross. He gave His life as the full payment for all of humanity's sin, iniquities and transgressions. Familiarize yourself with these passages of Scripture and use them in your plea: Isaiah 53; Galatians 3:13-14; Colossians 2:14-15.

5. Present the blood of Jesus as the acceptable sacrifice that satisfies the righteous requirements of a Holy God. It is also by means of the blood that we overcome the accuser, Satan, and take back any legal ground that had been given over to him.

    The Amplified translation of Isaiah 53:11 says, "He shall see the fruit of the travail of His soul and be satisfied; by His knowledge…shall My [uncompromisingly] righteous One, My Servant, justify many and make many righteous (upright and in right standing with God) for He shall bear their iniquities and their guilt [with the consequences, says the Lord]."

    With His blood Jesus made full payment for our sins, and His righteousness has been imputed to us. Because of the righteousness of Jesus that is given to us as believers, we can stand on that ground as righteous Abraham did in pleading the case of those who are not innocent. (See also Isaiah 53:5-6 and Revelation 12:11; Genesis 18:16-33.)

6. Plead for mercy. Be sure that you are someone who shows mercy in forgiving others for their trespasses against you. Being a merciful person qualifies your offspring to receive mercy from God. "Blessed are the merciful for they shall obtain mercy" (Matthew

5:7 KJV). Also, according to Psalm 37:26 KJV, the righteous are merciful and their seed is blessed.

7. As a Hopekeeper parent, rely on God's covenant that extends to your offspring. God is a generational God, and as we see in the case of Abraham, His covenant extends to our descendants. By faith in Jesus we are the seed of Abraham and partakers of his covenant blessings. We can ask for God's grace to bring our offspring into relationship with Him so that they also inherit the blessings of the even better covenant that Jesus has mediated for us. "Know therefore that the LORD your God is God; he is the faithful God, keeping his covenant of love to a thousand generations of those who love him and keep his commands" (Deuteronomy 7:9). (See also Galatians 3:7, 9.)

8. Bring witnesses from the Word of God. We know that God never changes. He is no respecter of persons, and He is the same yesterday, today, and forever. What He has done for others in the past He will do for you. His principles are unchangeable so you can rely on the precedent of His compassion, mercy and deliverance of others in pleading your case. (See Hebrews 13:8.)

9. Unite yourself with God's higher purposes on earth. We often do not think of this, but God is also seeking His own generation of righteous offspring on the earth for His Kingdom purposes. When we commit the lives of our young people to God for His higher purposes, He has a vested interest in seeing them delivered. The King James translation of Psalm 22:30-31 says, "A seed shall serve him; it shall be accounted to the Lord for a generation. They shall come, and shall declare his righteousness unto a people that shall be born, that he hath done this." We are pleading for God's generations, not just ours. (See also Isaiah 53:8; 1 Peter 2:9; Psalm 24:6.)

10. Remain confident in the mercy, faithfulness and unfailing love of the Supreme Judge of heaven.

A Sample Plea for God's Grace and Mercy

Sovereign Lord, Supreme Judge of heaven and earth, I approach your throne covered in the righteousness of Jesus Christ. I acknowledge and repent of all the ways in which we have sinned against you. I ask forgiveness and plead the blood of Jesus, with which He paid in full for all our transgressions, sins and iniquity.

I plead for mercy and grace, Great Judge, and ask that Your rich mercy be extended to _____ so that he/she might be delivered from the bondage of Satan. Let Your mercy triumph over judgment.

I ask that You would pour out Your grace upon _____ so that his/her heart will be turned to You in repentance. It is not Your will that any should perish, but that all should come to repentance. Bring _____ forth in righteousness as one who will serve Your Kingdom purposes on the earth. Let every one of Your good plans for his/her life be fulfilled.

Sovereign and Supreme Judge, I ask that You would judge the wicked one and banish him along with all his forces to the place You have assigned for them. I ask for a divine injunction against them so that _____ will never again be tormented or ensnared by them.

I make this plea not because of any good we have done, but because Your righteous Servant, Jesus, took every curse upon Himself, offered His life as a perfect sacrifice for our sin, and in His death and resurrection defeated the wicked one on our behalf. We ask that the victory of the cross and of the blood be applied now to every area of _____'s life.

We have repented, we stand on the ground of Jesus' provision, and we believe that by Your grace and mercy there is no reason why _____ should not be released from the imprisonment of the enemy, in Jesus' name. *Amen.*

Additional Plea (Hopekeeper Parents)

_____ is the seed of the righteous, and You have said that the seed of the righteous shall be delivered. By faith in Jesus, His righteousness has been imputed to me, and by Your covenant of peace that You have established with me and my descendants, I believe that this same righteousness has been imputed to my offspring.

You have also said that whoever calls on the name of the Lord will be saved, and that by believing on the Lord, I and my household will be saved. Thank You for making me a believer and for extending to my offspring the blessing of salvation, deliverance and wholeness.

Thank You for hearing our plea and for granting our petitions, in Jesus' name. *Amen.*

Supplementary Strategy #3: Speak Words of Blessing

This strategy is somewhat similar to the strategy of sending the Word, but it is distinct in many ways. The blessing strategy is based on Ephesians 1:3, which tells us that God the Father has blessed us in the heavenly realms with every spiritual blessing in Christ.

I encourage you to read the books in the Resource List by Terry and Melissa Bone for insights on how the spoken blessing impacts others, and to learn the spiritual art of crafting personalized blessings.

To help you get started, below you will find a summary of some distinct features of the spoken blessing as well as a sample blessing.

1. Ideally, the blessing should be spoken directly to the individual, but if you do not have the opportunity to speak face-to-face, do not hesitate to send it in the same way you send the Word. Special occasions such as birthdays are great opportunities, but there is no need to wait. You can speak or send a blessing anytime.
2. The blessing is an impartation of love, honor, value, and worth. It is conveyed through words spoken in the authority of God, our heavenly Father, from whom all blessing comes.
3. The blessing has the power to heal the souls of our young people from the effect of any word curses that might have intentionally or unintentionally been released over them.
4. The blessing will convey God's favor and enabling to help our young people achieve supernatural results in their lives. It

releases an anointing and empowerment for prosperity in all areas of life, and for divine protection.

5. Through the blessing we are able to impart to our young people an awareness of the unique identity and destiny God has designed for them and empower them to walk in it.

6. The blessing defies their present negative behaviors and lifestyles with an injection of hope for transformation and victory.

Be sensitive to the receptiveness and unique needs of the one to whom you are preparing to impart the blessing. Keep in mind that at certain times a hug and a sincere "I love you" may be all the blessing that he/she is prepared to receive.

A Sample Blessing

Today, _____, on behalf of your heavenly Father, and in His authority, I speak this blessing over your life.

I bless you as the beloved son/daughter of your heavenly Father, and I call you forth into the place of purpose and destiny that He has prepared for you. I bless your pathway to that destination.

As of this day, may it sink deep into your spirit, heart, and soul that you are an individual of great value and worth. Your heavenly Father's love for you makes you complete. You lack nothing!

I declare that you shall return from the land of the enemy. You shall not remain there, for there is hope for your future. May you be held in the palm of the hands of Almighty God, your heavenly Father. May He keep you from all evil, and may His face always be turned towards you.

I bless you with discernment, wisdom, and courage to find the way of escape that God has already prepared for you. I decree in the authority of Jesus' name that when the time is fully come, the power of the blood of Jesus shall break every snare, and you shall walk out of every bondage into the marvelous liberty of Christ. And it shall be as if you had never been ensnared.

With this blessing I declare that you shall not wander or die in the wilderness, but you will enter in and possess the Kingdom that God, your heavenly Father, prepared for you before the foundation of the earth. You will fulfill the purpose for which you were born.

I call you forth now as part of the generation that seeks after God and serves Him wholeheartedly. You will fulfill your potential, and you will do great exploits for the advancement of God's Kingdom.

With this blessing I put the name of the Lord upon you, as one belonging to God and empowered by Him. Know this day that you are blessed of the Lord with a blessing that cannot be reversed. As one whom God has blessed, you, _____, cannot be cursed. *Amen.*

An Extraordinary Opportunity – Rite of Passage

A rite of passage blessing at puberty is God's design to empower boys and girls as they physically transition into becoming young men and women.

In the Jewish culture this is accomplished by a special ceremony in which fathers bless their sons and daughters into adulthood. A boy experiencing this ceremony is traditionally called a *Bar Mitzvah,* meaning "Son of the Law" in Hebrew. Girls are called *Bat Mitzvah,* "Daughter of the Law."[1]

Many other cultures have similar practices to mark this major milestone. Unfortunately, our western culture has lost the awareness of the significance of a rite of passage from childhood to adulthood. I believe that our impartation of blessing at this critical juncture will save our young people from much of the confusion and crisis they have been experiencing.

We as Hopekeepers, in particular men and fathers, have an extraordinary opportunity to restore and institute God's intended plan to prepare our young people for adulthood. Churches and communities are recognizing the need to assist parents in this respect, and are establishing various types of rite of passage programs.[2]

The book in the Resource List by Craig Hill will give you an indepth understanding of what is involved in conducting a Christian rite of passage ceremony.[3] His book also includes a sample prayer and blessing for fathers to impart to their sons.

Other Supplementary Strategies

Pray through the night watch. This is what Lamentations 2:19 encourages us to do: "Arise, cry out in the night, as the watches of the night begin; pour out your heart like water in the presence of the Lord. Lift up your hands to him for the lives of your children."

You may pray through the night watch on your own or with others, but praying with others intensifies the results. We have an example of this in the deliverance of the Apostle Peter from prison in Acts 12:5-19. The very night that the angel delivered Peter, many had gathered together at the house of Mary, the mother of John, for a prayer night watch. In the same way, the Lord is able to send His angels to bring about the deliverance of our young people as we pray through the night watch.

Pray in the Spirit. We mentioned this dimension of prayer in an earlier chapter. Here I want to encourage you to make it a top personal priority to train and discipline yourself in following the lead of the Spirit of God as your engagement in this battle for young people intensifies. For this you must be strengthened with God's might in your spirit, so make Ephesians 3:16 one of your personal prayers. "Father, I pray that out of your glorious riches you would strengthen me with power through your Spirit in my inner being." (Personalized)

Your goal in this strategy is to become one who yields to and relies on the Holy Spirit. As you do this, you will tap into the wisdom of God, and the Holy Spirit will help you to establish prayer focus and priority. With the Holy Spirit guiding you in prayer, you will also have the assurance that you are praying the will of God. This is your guarantee for divine intervention.

Use your weapon of fasting more frequently. Fasting intensifies your prayer because it sharpens your spiritual senses. Fasting provides the discipline and training we need to operate in sync with the Holy Spirit and Jesus, our Commander in Chief. The fast is also one of the ways that we sacrifice our own lives (die to our own self lives and pleasures) so that our young people might live.

These next two strategies are for Hopekeeper parents.

Pray over their possessions. We may not have the opportunity to pray with our grown children, but if they are still living at home or if we have access to their possessions we can pray in their rooms and over their belongings as a point of contact. Anoint their possessions with oil as a symbol of the power of the Holy Spirit operating in their lives; apply the blood of Jesus by faith; declare to principalities and powers of darkness what the Word of God says concerning your offspring; and fill their environment with the presence of God through your prayers and songs of praise.

Sow a Seed for Breakthrough. Whatever good thing we make happen for others, God will make happen for us. That is a Wisdom Key I learnt from Mike Murdock some years ago. It is a powerful strategy that enables parents and other individuals to be actively engaged as part of the solution to the youth crisis.

While it may not be easy to think about someone else's crisis in the midst of a crisis with your own teen or young adult, it is an opportune time to invest or sow a seed for the restoration of other young people. This seed will in turn produce the harvest of a breakthrough for your son or daughter. This is how the Scriptures describe the strategy:

> Do not be deceived: God is not mocked. A man reaps what he sows. (Galatians 6:7)

> Knowing that whatever good anyone does, he will receive the same from the Lord.... (Ephesians 6:8)

So what do you have that you can sow as a seed? Your time, prayers and money are seeds that you can sow with the expectation that they will create or produce the desired harvest.

- You can volunteer your time to mentor a youth or to serve in an organization or ministry that is making a difference in the lives of youth.

- You can pray for other young people in crisis as well as the organizations and ministries that are reaching out to them. Our sons and daughters have friends who have gone astray. They may not have anyone praying for them, but we can pray for them, realizing that God desires their deliverance as much as He desires to deliver our offspring. God moves in mysterious ways, and to get to our offspring He may even choose to first turn the heart of one of their friends.
- You can sponsor a youth in a rehabilitation program or partner financially with organizations and ministries that are successfully restoring young people's lives.

The implications of the crisis we are dealing with extend far beyond just us and our family. It touches the very heart of God and His dominion on the earth. I trust that we will join forces and cry out to Him not only for our own offspring, but also for the young people in our neighborhood, in our city, in our nation, and in other nations of the world. This is God's battle; and when we get involved in His battle, He will get involved in ours.

FOCAL POINTS
FOR
SUPPLEMENTARY STRATEGIES

Record the date and specific strategies that you were impressed to focus on. Be faithful in using them until the Holy Spirit gives you a new focus. Also record any special thoughts that come to mind concerning each Focal Point.

DATE	REFERENCE NUMBER	THOUGHTS AND NOTES

Chapter Sixteen

Prayer, Blessing and a Word for God's Hopekeeper Warriors

Well done, faithful one! You have stayed with us and worked through all of the intervention strategies. In that respect you are a finisher. In another respect, however, your work has just begun, for much diligence will be required of you in applying what you now know.

Listen to the cry of the Spirit as we go forward:

Carry each other's burdens, and in this way you will fulfill the law of Christ. (Galatians 6:2)

Let us hold tightly without wavering to the hope we affirm, for God can be trusted to keep his promise. Let us think of ways to motivate one another to acts of love and good works. (Hebrews 10:23-24 NLT)

The prayer and blessing in this chapter are for us to pray and speak one for the other. As we do this, each Hopekeeper will be encircled and upheld by the prayers and blessings of many. This will help us to find supernatural joy and hope in the midst of our circumstances so that like the Apostle Paul, we can say, "Yes, and I will continue to rejoice, for I know that through your prayers and the help given by the Spirit of Jesus Christ, what has happened to me will turn out for my deliverance" (Philippians 1:19).

A Prayer for Fellow Hopekeeper Warriors

16.1 Lord, we thank You for each person You have called to Your army of Hopekeeper Warriors. Thank You for raising them up as faithful warriors to keep hope alive for their natural offspring as well as the offspring of others that You have entrusted to them.

We pray that they will all stand firm in faith, always abounding in this work of the Lord knowing that their labor is not in vain. May they be strong, courageous and confident in Your faithfulness and in Your power. Grant them a spirit of perseverance so that after they have done all they will receive what You have promised.

May they not be like the men of Ephraim who, though armed with bows, turned back in the day of battle. Rather, may they stand victoriously, clothed in Your whole armor and in Your strength against all the strategies and deceit of the devil.

Lord, cause Your mighty anointing of intercession to be upon each Hopekeeper so that they will give You no rest until Your purpose for their offspring, their families, their generation of young people, their nations, and Your Kingdom is accomplished. May they remain committed to You, Lord, and to this cause, knowing full well that they have an eternal reward with You.

We ask that You would impart to each one the Spirit of wisdom and of understanding, the Spirit of counsel and of power, the Spirit of knowledge and the fear of the Lord.

Father of compassion and God of all comfort, we ask You to comfort them so that they will be able to comfort others with the same comfort with which they have been comforted.

Banish all discouragement and cause every attack of the evil one against them to fail. Fill them with Your Holy Spirit and meet their every need. In Jesus' name we pray. Amen. (1 Corinthians 15:58; Hebrews 10:36; Psalm 78:9; Ephesians 6:10-11; Isaiah 62:7; Isaiah 11:1; 2 Corinthians 1:3-4)

Blessing Fellow Hopekeeper Warriors

16.2   We bless you with strength and courage as you wait on the Lord.

May your strength and courage be renewed daily as you hope in the Lord. May you soar on wings like eagles. May you run and not grow weary and may you walk and not faint. (Isaiah 40:31)

May you wait and hope for and expect the Lord. May you be brave and of good courage and let your heart be stout and enduring. Yes, may you wait for and hope for and expect the Lord. (Psalm 27:14 AMP)

16.3   We bless you with divine wisdom.

May you receive the Word of the Lord and treasure His commandments within you. May your ears be attentive to skilful and godly wisdom. May you cry out for insight and raise your voice for understanding. May you seek for wisdom as for silver, and search for skilful and godly wisdom as for hidden treasures, so that you may reverently fear the Lord and find the knowledge of God. May God's wisdom be within you, giving you counsel, sound knowledge, might, and power. (Proverbs 2:1-5; 8:14 AMP)

16.4   We bless you with the grace to persevere.

May the Lord bless you with His divine enabling to persevere to the end, knowing that after you have done the will of God you will receive what He has promised. May you never throw away your confidence, which will be richly rewarded. (Hebrews 10:35-36)

May you never grow weary in keeping hope alive and in doing good, knowing with confident assurance that in due season you will reap if you do not lose heart. (Galatians 6:9)

16.5   We bless you with your eternal reward.

May the LORD, the God of Israel, under whose wings you have come to take refuge, reward you fully for what you have done. (Ruth 2:12 NLT)

16.6   A blessing for answered prayers.

May the LORD answer you when you are in distress; may the name of the God of Jacob protect you. May he send you help from the sanctuary and grant you support from Zion. May He remember all your sacrifices and accept your burnt offerings. May He give you the desire of your heart and make all your plans succeed. We will shout for joy when you are victorious and will lift up our banners in the name of our God. May the LORD grant all your requests. (Psalm 20:1-5)

May the LORD remember His Word and His promise to you in which He has given you hope and may He cause them to be fulfilled. (Psalm 119:49)

16.7   A blessing for Hopekeeper, Parents and their offspring.

May the LORD richly bless both you and your children, giving you increase in every good thing. May you be blessed by the LORD, who made heaven and earth. And may it please the LORD to bless you with a family line of descendants who will be established in His presence forever. (Psalm 115:14-15 NLT; 2 Samuel 7:25-29)

16.8   The priestly blessing.

The LORD bless you and keep you; the LORD make his face shine upon you and be gracious to you; the LORD turn his face toward you and give you His peace. May the name of the LORD rest upon you, and may you be blessed indeed. (Numbers 6:24-27)

A Word from the Lord

There is a word from the Lord that He would have us hear as we go forward in this battle for our offspring, other young people, and the nations within them. May this word be to you a sweet refreshing not only today but in the days ahead.

I have called you, dear Hopekeeper, to walk through the door of hope that I have prepared for you. I speak to you as one who is a prisoner of hope. "As for you, because of the blood of my covenant with you, / I will free your prisoners from the waterless pit. / Return to your fortress [stay anchored in Jesus, your stronghold], O prisoners of hope; / even now I announce that I will restore twice as much to you" (Hosea 2:15; Zechariah 9:11-12).

I will indeed bring your offspring and the others for whom you travail from the far off places to which they have wandered, the ends of the earth as it were, and establish them in righteousness for my name's sake. I will satisfy the desires of your heart. I will do as I have promised. I will give you the nations as your inheritance and the ends of the earth as your possession. (Psalm 2:8)

Arise! Gird yourself with my strength, O mighty warrior. Be diligent, strong and courageous. Fight! Fight for your sons and daughters! As Nehemiah, my servant, said to the people who were rebuilding the walls of Jerusalem in ancient times, "Don't be afraid of them [the enemy]. Remember the Lord, who is great and awesome, and fight for your brothers, your sons and your daughters, your wives and your homes" (Nehemiah 4:14).

These dear ones for whom you are fighting belong to Me. They are Mine, for I have fashioned them for My glory. And when I have brought deliverance to them and given you rest, do not forget those who are yet to come into their season of rest. As Moses said to the fighting men of the tribes that had taken their inheritance on the east side of the Jordan, "You are to help your brothers until the LORD gives them rest, as he has done for you, and until they too have taken possession of the land that the LORD your God is giving them" (Joshua 1:14b-15a).

I require of you that you arm yourself with the same mind as those fighting men and say like them, we will not turn back until everyone has received their inheritance. (Numbers 32:18)

Faint not in the heat of the battle, for the war has already been won. The battle is not yours, but Mine. Stand firm and you will see the deliverance that I the Lord will bring you. I will fight for you. (Exodus 14:13)

I have left you My peace to guard your mind and heart. And the peace I give is not like the peace the world gives. So do not be troubled or afraid. (John 14:27)

Trust in Me and keep your hope alive. Look not at the struggles of each day, but fix your eyes on the joy set before you. Do not lose heart. Look not on what is seen but on what is unseen, for what is seen is temporary, but what is unseen is eternal. Set your heart now to persevere, for the race is not to the swift or the battle to the strong. It is for those who endure to the end. (2 Corinthians 4:16-18; Ecclesiastes 9:11)

Be encouraged, for I say to you that not one, not even one of your words spoken in faith on My behalf will fall to the ground or return without accomplishing what it is sent to do. I will indeed watch over them and bring them to fulfillment. My covenant with you will not fail. (Isaiah 55:11; Jeremiah 1:12)

Persevere! An eternal weight of glory awaits you that exceeds anything you could imagine. Let nothing rob you of your eternal reward. I cannot fail. In My kindness I will not fail you, and I will not let you fail. Trust and hope to the end!

FOCAL POINTS
FOR PRAYERS, BLESSING AND A WORD
FOR GOD'S HOPEKEEPER WARRIORS

Record the date and reference number of the prayers and blessing that you were impressed to focus on, and note any Focal Points relating to the Word from the Lord. Be faithful in using them until the Holy Spirit gives you a new focus. Also record any special thoughts that come to mind concerning each Focal Point.

DATE	REFERENCE NUMBER	THOUGHTS AND NOTES

Chapter Seventeen

Safeguards for Young and Unborn Children

W hen I started writing this book, I had mature parents in mind as its primary audience. My commission from the Lord was to bring them hope for the restoration of their grown children whose lives are in crisis. It soon became clear, however, that I needed to include strategies that would help to safeguard young children from the present pitfalls.

It is heartbreaking to hear how many children are being drawn into evil at younger and younger ages. But we need not watch helplessly as Satan ensnares the younger generation.

New and prospective parents have the opportunity to stop Satan in his tracks and reverse the early patterns of evil among young children. By implementing safeguard strategies, they can prevent or avert the trouble into which many of our teens and young adults have fallen.

God's Good Plans

One of the things that must be clear in our minds is that the crisis into which our grown children have fallen is not God's plan for their lives. Their defilement and the long hard battle to restore them is heartbreaking, not only for us but for God as well. While He is able by His sovereign power to turn the evil they have experienced into good, His ideal is for our children to fulfill His good plans for their lives without having to go the roundabout route.

God's good plan for our children is that from an early age they would know Him, know their true identity and the purpose for which they were born, and represent God's Kingdom. This is not just wishful thinking. It is attainable, for with God all things are possible. We have many examples from the Scriptures, and since God does not change, we know that He can accomplish in our time what He did in the past.

Josiah, for example, was a boy who became the king of Judah at the age of eight and reigned as an exceptional leader.

He did what was pleasing in the LORD's sight and followed the example of his ancestor David. He did not turn away from doing what was right. (2 Kings 22:2 NLT)

Never before had there been a king like Josiah, who turned to the LORD with all his heart and soul and strength, obeying all the laws of Moses. And there has never been a king like him since. (2 Kings 23:25 NLT)

What a testimony! We also have Samuel who grew up in the temple and ministered to the Lord from his very early childhood days. In spite of the evil practices of the sons of Eli, Samuel remained faithful. "But Samuel, though he was only a boy, served the LORD" (1 Samuel 2:18 NLT).

New and prospective parents have the opportunity to stop satan in his tracks and reverse the early patterns of evil among young children.

Daniel and the other three Hebrew teens who were taken into Babylonian captivity are other well-known examples of young people who remained undefiled even in the midst of adversity, threats, and temptations.

I believe with all my heart that even in the midst of our crooked and perverse generation, we are able to raise children who will stand for righteousness, represent God's Kingdom, and walk in their destiny from an early age.

A Word for the Next Generation of Parents

My message to the next generation of parents is that many of us missed it but they do not have to. They need not make the same mistakes that many of us from the older generations made. We who have learnt from our mistakes have a responsibility before God to pass on to them the wisdom and hope that we have received from the Lord. This chapter of the book is a step in that direction.

A Golden Opportunity for Grandparents

If you are a Hopekeeper parent whose teenage or young adult son or daughter is in trouble or headed for trouble, I want you to know that a golden opportunity awaits you with your young and future grandchildren.

Allow the Lord to turn the pain you have experienced, even your mistakes and regrets, into a passion for safeguarding the next generation of your descendants from Satan's assault. You are a seasoned warrior who has been trained in the trenches. The honor of "grand" that has been bestowed upon you in your title of grandparent is fitting—you have earned it!

The skills you have gained in your many battles have given you an edge against the enemy. In this round of the warfare you have the opportunity to shift from being on the defensive to being on the offensive.

I am not advocating that you take over the parenting of your grandchildren. That is their parents' job. Your role is that of a coach or consultant. You provide encouragement and give advice only when solicited. However, you now know the divine intervention strategies that are available to you for situations over which you do not have direct influence. God has given you the authority to pray, decree, declare, and proclaim His will into situations that are within your spiritual sphere of influence. Your descendants, even those yet to be born—children, grandchildren, and their children—are at the top of that list.

The strategies in this chapter are as much for you as a Hopekeeper parent with grown children as they are for new and prospective parents. We trust that you will have an opportunity to introduce them to the parents of your grandchildren and that you will be able to join forces with them in using the strategies.

Even if there is resistance, remember that as a grandparent God's covenant with you extends to your grandchildren. In the realm of the spirit, you have the right of influence over them that satanic forces have to respect. Honor your responsibility before God to stand in the gap and implement the divine intervention strategies on behalf of your grandchildren. I trust that you will be faithful to the Lord in praying for the nations that will come out of the loins and wombs of your descendants in the years to come.

The Battle Is the Same

Whether we are dealing with grown or young children, the battle is essentially the same. We are engaged in warfare against the enemy for the life of our offspring, regardless of their age. The weaponry, the preparation, and the warfare strategies are therefore quite similar.

The Word of God is both a defensive and offensive weapon against the enemy. Like the intervention strategies for grown offspring, the preventative or safeguard strategies for the young ones are also based on the Word of God.

In this chapter we will be presenting six preventative or safeguard strategies. Some of the principles have been presented already, so they are not entirely new. The main difference is in the timing of their application.

The First Six Years Are the Key

The earlier the better! That is the main idea when it comes to preventative or safeguard strategies. In fact, prospective parents gain a major advantage over the enemy when they start using these strategies even before conception. It is never too early, for as the old sayings go, prevention is better than cure, and a stitch in time saves nine.

The earlier the better! That is the main idea when it comes to preventative or safeguard strategies.

The first six years are a child's foundational years, and what parents do in these early years is a major factor in determining the outcome of later years. Many parents have missed this window of opportunity, however, because of a lack of understanding of how the child functions during this period. A very young child does not process information intellectually the way an adult does, so there is no need to wait for the brain faculties to develop before we introduce God's Word to him or her.

Now, let's start examining our safeguard strategies. First, a strategy concerning the parent before we move on to the child.

Safeguard Strategy #1: Prepare Yourself

Parents know how to make the material preparations for the arrival of a newborn. Few are aware, however, that they also need to prepare themselves. The principle behind this strategy is that as parents we must first be what our children are to become.

In Judges chapter thirteen, when the angel announced the birth of Samson, we see that the angel did not only give instructions concerning the child. He also gave specific instructions for the mother to prepare for the conception. "Now see to it that you drink no wine or other fermented drink and that you do not eat anything unclean, because you will conceive and give birth to a son" (Judges 13:4–5a).

As parents we must first be what our children are to become.

This strategy of parental preparation is necessary because of how the law of reproduction works. We reproduce after our own kind. We reproduce what we are, and what is in us passes on to our offspring.

Parents pass on more than their physical features and characteristics to their children. They also reproduce their predisposition to certain weaknesses and strengths. Moreover, the legacy that the child inherits is not only what comes directly from its parents. A child actually comes into the world carrying the cumulative legacy of past generations. This is a mixture of both positives and negatives, and the mixture continues until someone in the family line goes before God to put an end to the negative traits.

Because of the effects of sin on humanity, we all have patterns of weaknesses in our family line that we would rather not see reproduced in our children. God has made a way to stop their progression and that is what this preparation strategy is all about.

Here are some steps that prospective parents can take to prepare for conception:

1. Take an honest inventory of any personal or ancestral weaknesses that you do not want to see manifested in your offspring.
2. Confess and repent of them before God. Put your faith in Jesus' sacrifice on the cross to redeem you and your offspring out of every curse, and ask God to cut off the progression of these evil patterns. It is important that prospective parents gain freedom over areas of personal weaknesses, for whatever we overcome in our own lives is less likely to be passed on to our offspring. (You may wish to review the repentance prayers in Chapters 9 and 11 for this preparatory step.)
3. Ask God to bless your offspring so that they will inherit only the generational blessings that He had intended for them to receive.
4. Wives, seek God for the cleansing and healing of your womb so that it is ready for the life that the Spirit of God will conceive and incubate there.
5. Husbands, consecrate to God the seed of life that is within your loins and ask God to bless it and make it holy unto himself.

When we read of Jesus, the Messiah, coming from the ancestral line of Rahab, the prostitute, we can believe with confidence that God is in the business of recreating wombs and redeeming generational legacies.

Safeguard Strategy #2: Dedicate Your Child to the Lord

With respect to new and unborn children, our model for this strategy is Hannah in the book of First Samuel, chapter one. After being childless for many years, Hannah prayed for a son and promised that she would return him to the Lord if her prayer was answered. Hannah followed through on her promise and dedicated her son Samuel to the Lord for a lifetime of service. Samuel became a great servant of God, serving as a judge, prophet and priest.

As a small child, Samuel started serving God in the temple under Eli the priest. But Eli's sons were very corrupt and did much evil in the sight of God. In that environment, Samuel could easily have become defiled and be led astray. However, he was safeguarded and preserved because Hannah had dedicated him wholly unto the Lord.

For this strategy of dedication to be effective, it is necessary to understand that it involves much more than having a pastor pray God's blessing of protection over a child.

From Hannah's example we learn certain principles about what is involved in dedicating a child to the Lord.

1. The dedication of a child to the Lord is a covenant of trust in which parents acknowledge God's ownership of the child's life and their responsibility as stewards.
2. The dedication of the child is incomplete without the parents also dedicating themselves to the Lord. In dedicating Samuel, Hannah also dedicated her entire life and future to God. She committed herself to doing her part in seeing God's purpose for Samuel's life fulfilled.
3. Dedicating a child is letting go of what we treasure most so that the child's life can continue to be shaped by God's hand. Hannah wanted a child more than anything else in the world, yet she was willing to give him back to the Lord. In return, the Lord took charge of Samuel's life and blessed Hannah with three other sons and two daughters.
4. The dedication of a child to God requires the ongoing renewal of the covenant. As humans it is quite easy to take back what we have put into the hands of God. I believe that Hannah renewed her covenant each year as she went to the temple for the annual sacrifice and brought along a robe for Samuel.

Parents can stand on 2 Timothy 1:12 in applying the dedication strategy: "...I know whom I have believed, and am convinced that he is able to guard what I have entrusted to him for that day."

Safeguard Strategy #3: Plant the Word of God in Your Child's Heart

The strategy of praying and declaring the Word of God on behalf of unborn and young children is just as critical as it is for grown children. When it comes to the young and unborn child, however, parents have the opportunity to do much more. They can plant the Word directly into the child's heart.

We said earlier that timing is the key factor in the application of these safeguard strategies, and for this particular strategy of planting the Word in the heart, timing is of the essence. It must be started before the child is capable of showing resistance or able to move around on its own.

To understand this strategy we need to look at the parable of the sower as told by Jesus in Mark 4:3-20. In this parable Jesus speaks of a farmer who sowed seeds that fell on four different kinds of ground: by the wayside, on rocky places, among thorns, and on good soil. Only the seeds that fell on the good soil were able to take root and produce a fruitful harvest. The seed in the parable is the Word of God, and the different soil represents the condition of the heart that receives the Word.

Of course, we are speaking here of the spiritual heart—the center or core of a person's being where all conscious and unconscious memories are stored, starting at conception. The heart is the source from which good or evil is later manifested in a person's life. Proverbs 4:23 therefore calls it the "wellspring of life."

Because of the sin nature inherited from Adam, the inclination of the heart is evil even from childhood, as Genesis 8:21 tells us. However, the seed of the Word of God is powerful; and if it is sown continually into a heart from conception, it is able to reconstitute that heart for good and save the soul. It will change the orientation of the heart away from evil, reconstitute it for good, and establish a foundation of real identity truths that will, in adolescence and later years, safeguard against the experimentation that Satan has used to ensnare our young people. (See James 1:21.)

I believe that this is the most powerful safeguard strategy that new and prospective parents have at their disposal.

Here are the key principles concerning this strategy of planting the Word of God in the child's heart:

1. The heart of a young child is good ground. In fact, the younger a child is the better will be the condition of the soil of its heart to receive the Word of God.

2. The Word of God will grow deep and permanent roots in the heart of a very young child because of the limited influence of evil upon its heart. No "thorns" are present to choke out the Word of God. The deeper the roots go into the soil of the heart, the stronger they are; and the stronger the roots are, the higher will be the spiritual growth that is produced in the child's life.

3. A young child absorbs from its environment through a process that is not dependent on the development of its intellectual faculties. The planting of the seed of the Word of God into the heart of a child can therefore begin at conception.

4. Planting the seed of the Word of God into the heart of very young children enables them to build up their own defense mechanism against the snares of the enemy in later years. In the words of Mark 4:17, they will have "real [or firm] root in themselves" (AMP, NAS).

5. A young child's heart that is filled with the Word of God is a faith-filled heart. As he/she grows to maturity, the child will choose the way of the *Word* rather than the way of the *world*. The child will have a strong foundation upon which to start building biblical values in later childhood that will insulate him or her against worldly ideas and teachings. The Word seeds planted in the child's heart will produce a harvest after its own kind in later years.

I believe this strategy of planting God's Word in a child's heart at an early age is the secret to parents not having to worry about their children's salvation and their walk with the Lord in later years. Their foundation and orientation would have already been set. It is also the secret to their growing up with a passion for the Word of God. The Word will be so firmly planted in them that they will grow up speaking "the language of heaven." It will be like "second nature" to them. Hallelujah!

So just how does one plant the Word into the heart of an unborn child or infant? Simply place a hand upon the womb or on the child and read particular passages of Scripture aloud. It does not matter whether the child is asleep or awake. Remember it is the child's spirit that will receive the words that are being spoken. Do not be distracted by the absence of a response on the part of the child. It is the Holy Spirit who will actually plant the Word in the child's heart and cause it to grow, so pray for the help of the Holy Spirit before and after your speaking.

Below you will find some "Word seeds" to get you started. However, I encourage you to rely on the Holy Spirit to provide you with an abundant supply of the Word for your child. Second Corinthians 9:10 says that He "supplies seed to the sower." Each child is fashioned uniquely by God, and the Holy Spirit knows exactly what each one needs. As you stay in the Word yourself, He will guide you and supply the exact "seed" that you need for your child at different times. Many of the prayers, declarations and decrees from earlier chapters can also be adapted as "seeds" for planting in the young child's heart.

We have prefaced each one with "my son/daughter," but it is best to specify your child's name. Also feel free to substitute other terms of endearment such as "my child" or "beloved one."

My son/daughter, in a humble, gentle, and modest spirit receive and welcome the Word which implanted and rooted in your heart contains the power to save your soul. (James 1:21 AMP)

My son/daughter, accept my words and store up my commands

within you. Turn your ear to wisdom and apply your heart to understanding. Call out for insight and cry aloud for understanding. Look for it as for silver, and search for it as for hidden treasure. Then you will understand the fear of the Lord and find the knowledge of God. For the Lord gives wisdom, and from his mouth come knowledge and understanding. (Proverbs 2:1-6)

My son/daughter, wisdom will enter your heart and knowledge will be pleasant to your soul. (Proverbs 2:10)

My son/daughter, apply your heart to instruction, and your ears to words of knowledge. (Proverbs 23:12)

My son/daughter, you will walk in the ways of good men and keep to the paths of the righteous. (Proverbs 2:20)

My son/daughter, do not forget my teaching, but keep my commands in your heart, for they will prolong your life many years and bring you prosperity. Let love and faithfulness never leave you; bind them around your neck, write them on the tablet of your heart. Then you will win favor and a good name in the sight of God and man. (Proverbs 3:1-4)

My son/daughter, trust in the LORD with all your heart and lean not on your own understanding; in all your ways acknowledge Him, and He will make your paths straight. Do not be wise in your own eyes; fear the Lord and shun evil. This will bring health to your body and nourishment to your bones. (Proverbs 3:5-8)

My son/daughter, you will have singleness of heart and action, so that you will always fear the Lord for your own good and the good of your children after you. (Jeremiah 33:39)

My son/daughter, I call you forth as the generation of those who seek the Lord; who inquire of and for Him and of necessity require Him. You are the generation of those who seek His face. So lift up your head. Lift up your gates and let the King of glory come in, the Lord strong and mighty, the Lord mighty in battle. (Psalm 24:6-7)

My son/daughter, you shall serve the LORD and tell of the Lord to the next generation. You shall be strong and do great exploits in the Kingdom of God. (Psalm 22:30; Daniel 11:32b)

My son/daughter, I say unto you that you shall be unto the Lord as an unbridled colt, one who shall never be held by the reins of the devil, and upon whom no man shall sit. But you are one wholly set apart unto the Lord for His purposes. For before the Lord formed you in the womb He knew you, and before you were born He set you apart. He appointed you as a prophet to the nations. (Mark 11:2; Jeremiah 1:5)

My son/daughter, you will hide the Word of God in your heart so that you will not sin against Him. (Psalm 119:11)

My son/daughter, the Word of God will be a lamp to your feet and a light to your path. (Psalm 119:105)

My son/daughter, you will be taught by the Lord, and great will be your peace. In righteousness you will be established. Tyranny will be far from you; you will have nothing to fear. Terror will be far removed; it will not come near you. (Isaiah 54:13-14)

My son/daughter, God's covenant is with you and His Spirit is on you. His words that He has put in your mouth will not depart from your mouth, or from the mouths of your children, or from the mouths of their descendants from this time on and forever. (Isaiah 59:21)

My son/daughter, the Lord your God will circumcise your heart so that you may love Him with all your heart and with all your soul, and live. (Deuteronomy 30:6)

My son/daughter, the Lord has poured His Spirit and His blessing upon you. You shall spring up like grass in a meadow, like poplar trees by flowing streams. You shall declare, 'I belong to the Lord,' and you shall call yourself by His name. (Isaiah 44:3-5)

My son/daughter, I say unto you that you shall be mighty and blessed in the earth. You are the head and not the tail, above only and never beneath. The favor of the Lord is upon you and His wisdom is within you. Everything that you set your hands to shall prosper. (Psalm 112:2; Deuteronomy 28:13; Psalm 5:12)

Safeguard Strategy #4: Speak Prophetically to Your Child

This strategy is related to the last one, for it also involves speaking forth

God's Word. However, speaking prophetically goes beyond speaking specific Scriptures. It involves speaking forth God's purposes and will for that child's life. The goal of this strategy is to help the child understand from a very early age that he or she holds a unique place in God's plans.

Here are some principles and examples concerning this strategy:

1. The main requirement for this strategy to work is for new and prospective parents to earnestly seek God for Him to reveal the specific purpose for which their child is being sent to the earth.

2. Being alert to the condition and needs of the nation in which they live and the present needs in the Kingdom of God, new and prospective parents have the opportunity to covenant with God to be part of the solution through the children they bring forth. As Dr. Patricia Morgan states in her book, *How to Raise Children of Destiny,* "Whenever a nation is in trouble, God causes a deliverer to be born!"[1]

   Again we learn from Hannah's example. She did not just ask God for a child. She asked for a son. Knowing the problems with Eli's sons in the temple at the time, Hannah desired a son who would become part of the solution. That, I believe, was her reason for bringing him back to live in the temple. This was early apprenticeship for his destiny. I believe she would also have prepared him for that destiny by prophesying over him in those years before he was weaned and brought to Eli.

3. Parents need the gift of discernment. In the account of Moses' birth we have an example of this principle. In a wicked plot to stop the Hebrew slaves from becoming more powerful than the Egyptians, the king of Egypt had ordered that all boys born to Hebrew women be killed. But the Bible tells us that Moses' mother perceived that he was a "special" child, so she defied the king's orders and kept him hidden. (See Exodus 1:15-2:10) As she nursed him, Moses' mother must have rehearsed to him the bondage that her people were in and his destiny as their

deliverer. Years later Moses fulfilled his destiny in delivering the children of Israel out of Egypt.

4. When Proverbs 22:6 speaks of training the child in the way he or she should go, it involves much more than physical discipline. The Amplified Bible translation of that verse gives us some insight: "Train up a child in the way he should go [and **in keeping with his individual gift or bent**], and when he is old he will not depart from it" (emphasis added). It requires that parents discern God's purpose for the child's life, and the gifts and abilities that He has designed into the child. Then it requires that they nurture the child accordingly so that in later years the child will bloom to his/her full potential as God intended.

5. Parents need to carefully choose names for their children that reflect a meaningful destiny. In a simple way, each calling or speaking of that name becomes a prophetic declaration and reinforcement of the meaning and destiny that it embodies.

In Luke chapter one, we have an excellent example of a father speaking prophetically concerning his son's destiny. Zechariah had been struck with dumbness for the duration of Elizabeth's pregnancy to safeguard the child against any negative speaking by his father. But now at the naming of John the Baptist, Zechariah's speech was restored and he spoke forth the child's destiny for the child, his mother, and others to hear.

"And you, my child, will be called a prophet of the Most High;
    for you will go on before the Lord to prepare the way for him,
to give his people the knowledge of salvation
    through the forgiveness of their sins,
because of the tender mercy of our God,
    by which the rising sun will come to us from heaven
to shine on those living in darkness
    and in the shadow of death,

to guide our feet into the path of peace." (Luke 1:76-79)

May the anointing that was upon Zechariah be upon the new generation of parents, enabling them to speak forth prophecies that will safeguard their children from a purposeless life in later years.

Safeguard Strategy #5: Bless Your Child's Identity and Destiny

The blessing, as we pointed out in chapter fifteen, is an impartation of love, honor, value, and worth through intentionally spoken words. The blessing also conveys God's favor and enabling into a person's life.

Your ultimate objective will be to impart a sense of identity and destiny that will enable your child to grow up knowing his or her true worth, significance and purpose on the earth. According to Craig Hill, the spoken family blessing is God's "ancient path" by which He intended these two key qualities of identity and destiny to be imparted at crucial times in a person's life.[2]

From the early years of Jesus' life, we see that God's intent is for children to be blessed at each major stage of development:

- Mary, the mother of Jesus, welcomed (blessed) Him at conception by her response to the angel: "Be it unto me according to thy word" (Luke 1:38 KJV). She was basically saying, I welcome this child that shall be conceived in my womb.
- Elizabeth blessed Jesus in the womb when Mary visited her shortly after the conception.
- The shepherds blessed Him at His birth.
- Simeon blessed Jesus as a baby when Mary and Joseph brought Him to the temple when He was forty days old to present Him to the Lord.
- The wise men blessed Him when they visited Him with gifts. (See Luke 1:42, 2:8-20, 28-35; Matthew 2:1-12.)

Knowledge of the blessing that had been lost to many generations of parents is now available to us, so new parents have the opportunity of blessing their children at each stage of development.

In their books on the blessing, Terry and Melissa Bone outline the seven major life stages at which a special impartation of the blessing is needed: at conception, during pregnancy, at birth, in childhood, in the teen years, in adulthood, and in the senior years. The first four stages are critical for safeguarding children from the experimentation and costly detours that could produce crisis in later years.

To assist you in crafting the blessing for these crucial stages, we have provided a brief summary below of what the blessing emphasizes at the stages from conception to childhood.

1. At conception the blessing welcomes with love and acceptance the newly arrived spirit of the child to his or her place in the earth. It affirms the child's unique value and God's choice for him or her to be conceived at this particular time for a unique purpose. The best start that a mother can give to her child is to receive the news of her pregnancy with acceptance, as this will safeguard her child against early seeds of rejection.

2. During pregnancy the blessing embraces the child with the assurance of his or her safety and security. It safeguards against detachment and against seeds of fear and anxiety being planted in the child's heart. Words of blessing spoken during pregnancy also release creative power for the completion of God's handiwork in perfectly fashioning the child's being (spirit, soul, and body).

3. At birth the blessing again expresses love and acceptance, including acceptance of the child's gender, which in many instances will be known for the first time. The blessing welcomes the child as a gift to his or her particular family, and assures the child of God's faithfulness in providing for his or her needs, continued development and protection. The blessing at birth also includes a blessing of the name chosen for the child.

4. During childhood the blessing is an empowerment for the child

to develop in every area (spiritually, socially, mentally, physically, emotionally, and morally) as God intended. The blessing conveys words of honor, love and acceptance for the development of his or her sense of being and well-being. It also conveys to the child the divine capacity to put his/her trust in the Lord and start developing relationships of trust with others. At each childhood birthday or other special occasion, the blessing affirms the child's worth, and calls forth the potential and special abilities with which the child has been uniquely endowed.

Children who are blessed from the early stages of life have the advantage of progressing confidently in the discovery of their true identity and the fulfillment of the special destiny that God has designed for them.

In addition to speaking blessing at each stage of your child's development, we encourage you to speak life-giving words to your child at all times so that the harvest produced from his/her life in later years will be a harvest of righteousness for the glory of God.

May you set a guard over your own heart, over your mouth, and keep watch over the door of your lips so that you speak and do only what is good and beneficial that it may impart grace and strength to your child.

Safeguard Strategy # 6: Stay Focused on the Heart

Whatever you accomplish by the strategy of planting the Word of God in your child's heart will be sustained by staying focused on his or her heart throughout the childhood and adolescent years.

One key area in which this is essential is in the area of discipline. Many socially accepted methods of disciplining aim at controlling behavior but never deal with the condition of the heart. We now understand quite clearly, however, that behavior, words, actions and attitudes are products of an individual's heart. (See Proverbs 4:23; Matthew 12:34b-35.)

Staying focused on the heart does not excuse or overlook inappropriate behavior. It means that in disciplining your child you seek to discern the real issue that is underlying the behavior and get at the root of it in the heart.

The goal is always to instruct the child in ways that will keep the heart oriented towards God. This goal remains a priority even when practical disciplinary action is being taken.

Your maintenance of a relationship with your child that reflects the sincere love of Father-God and His mercy will keep the child open to the correcting influence of God's Word and grace upon his or her heart. As you pray and trust the Lord for parental discernment, He will help you to uncover the hidden things of your child's heart and will give you the wisdom to apply the appropriate discipline.

May you remain faithful in applying these safeguard strategies. As you do so, I believe that God will indeed honor your faithfulness and preserve your child in later years. "To the faithful, God shows Himself faithful (Psalm 18:25)." Through your faithfulness, may He also secure for Himself a generation that seeks after His face.

Keep your hope alive!

APPLICATION POINTS
FOR
SAFEGUARDS FOR YOUNG AND UNBORN CHILDREN

1. What do you say are three major advantages of these early safe-guard strategies?
2. Why is timing of utmost importance in applying these strate-gies?
3. Why is it not necessary to wait for the development of the child's intellectual faculties to begin applying safeguard strategies?
4. Write a few words or a sentence that expresses your under-standing of the benefits, advantage and purpose of each of the six safeguard strategies.
   a. Preparing yourself
   b. Dedicating your child to the Lord
   c. Planting the Word of God in your child's heart
   d. Speaking prophetically to your child
   e. Blessing your child's identity and destiny
   f. Staying focused on the heart

END NOTES

CHAPTER 1

1. See the Support Services section for more information on rehabilitation services.

CHAPTER 2

1. James Richards, *Grace: The Power to Change* (New Kensington, PA: Whitaker House, 1993), 22

2. Creflo A. Dollar Jr., *The Power of God's Grace* (College Park, GA: Creflo Dollar Publications, 1997), 3

CHAPTER 4

1. Mike Shreve, *Our Glorious Inheritance: The Revelation of the Titles of the Children of God,* Volume 6 (Taylors, SC: Deeper Revelation Books, 1991), 3

CHAPTER 5

1. Charles Capps, *God's Creative Power Will Work For You* (Tulsa, OK: Harrison House, Inc., 1976), 29

CHAPTER 8

1. Myles Munroe, *The Principle of Fatherhood: Priority, Position, and the Role of the Male* (Lanham, MD: Pneuma Life Publishing, 2001), 57

2. Linda Mintle, *Breaking Free from a Negative Self-Image* (Lake Mary, FL: Charisma House, 2002), 39

3. This word concerning being at war was spoken in the context of a judgment against Asa, king of Judah. We will, however, consider it a call to war in the present context of God's conscription order.

4. Larry S. Clark, Copyright © 1993.

CHAPTER 11

1. Webster's Encyclopedic Unabridged Dictionary of the English Language.

2. Gage Canadian Dictionary.

3. Joel Osteen, *Your Best Life Now: 7 Steps to Living at Your Full Potential* (New York, NY: Warner Faith, 2004), 194-195

CHAPTER 15

1. Craig Hill, *Bar Barakah: A Parent's Guide to a Christian Bar Mitzvah* (Littleton, CO: Family Foundations International, 1998), 9

2. One such program is the Rite of Passage Experience (ROPE) in the Greater Toronto Area that targets single mothers and their sons. ROPE is designed to assist young black male teenagers lead lives free of violence. Visit www.adventfamilyservices.org/aboutrope.html for more information.

3. The name Craig Hill suggests for those experiencing the Christian equivalent of the Jewish ceremony is *Bar Barakáh* or *Bat Barakáh*, "Son of the Blessing" or "Daughter of the Blessing" respectively.

CHAPTER 17

1. Patricia Morgan, *How to Raise Children of Destiny: Imparting Purpose from Generation to Generation* (New Kensington, PA: Whitaker House, 2003), 22

2. Craig Hill, *The Ancient Paths* (Littleton, CO: Family Foundations International, 1992).

Resource List

Bone, Terry and Melissa. *The Power of Blessing: Discovering your True Identity and Destiny in Christ.* Canada, 2005

Bone, Terry. *The Blessing Handbook: How to Give a Blessing to Anyone Who Needs One.* Burlington, ON: Crossroads Christian Communications, 2007

Coulter, B. Kay. *Victim/Victor: It's Your Choice.* Longwood, FL: Xulon Press, 2002

Capps, Charles. *The Tongue: A Creative Force.* Tulsa, OK: Harrison House, Inc., 1976

Capps, Charles. *God's Creative Power Will Work for You.* Tulsa, OK: Harrison House, Inc., 1976

Frangipane, Francis. *This Day We Fight!: Breaking the Bondage of a Passive Spirit.* Grand Rapids, MI: Chosen Books, 2005

Hickey, Marilyn. *Breaking Generational Curses: Overcoming the Legacy of Sin in Your Family.* Tulsa, OK: Harrison House, Inc., 2000

Hill, Craig. *Bar Barakah: A Parent's Guide to a Christian Bar Mitzvah.* Littleton, CO: Family Foundations International, 1998

Larson, Scott and Brendtro, Larry. *Reclaiming your Prodigal Sons and Daughters: A Practical Approach to Connecting With Youth in Crisis.* Bloomington, IN: National Educational Services, 2000

Linamen, Karen Scalf. *Parent Warrior: Protecting Your Children Through Prayer.* Grand Rapids, MI: Fleming H. Revell, 1993

Mintle, Linda. *Breaking Free from a Negative Self-Image.* Lake Mary, FL: Charisma House, 2002

Morgan, Patricia. *The Battle for the Seed: Spiritual Strategy to Preserve Our Children.* New Kensington, PA: Whitaker House, 2003

Morgan, Patricia. *How to Raise Children of Destiny: Imparting Purpose from Generation to Generation.* New Kensington, PA: Whitaker House, 2003

Munroe, Myles. *Understanding the Purpose and Power of Prayer: Earthly Licence for Heavenly Interference.* New Kensington, PA: Whitaker House, 2002

Munroe, Myles. *The Principle of Fatherhood: Priority, Position and the Role of the Male.* Lanham, MD: Pneuma Life Publishing, 2001

Munroe, Myles and Burrows, David. *Kingdom Parenting.* Shippensburg, PA: Destiny Image, 2007

Nichols, Fern. *Every Child Needs a Praying Mom.* Grand Rapids, MI: Zondervan, 2003

Omartian, Stormie. *The Power of a Praying Parent.* Eugene, OR: Harvest House Publishers, 1995

Scott, Buddy. *Relief for Hurting Parents: How to Fight for the Lives of Your Teenagers.* Lake Jackson, TX: Allon Publishing, 1997

Sumrall, Lester. *The Names of God.* New Kensington, PA: Whitaker House, 1982

Sheets, Dutch. *Authority in Prayer: Praying with Power and Purpose.* Bloomington, MN: Bethany House, 2006

Sherrer, Quinn and Garlock, Ruthanne. *Praying Prodigals Home: Taking Back What The Enemy Has Stolen.* Ventura, CA: Regal Books, 2000

Smith, Eddie and Alice. *The Advocates: How to Plead the Case of Others in Prayer.* Lake Mary, FL: Charisma House, 2001

Tripp, Tedd. *Shepherding a Child's Heart.* Wapwallopen, PA: Shepherd Press, 1995

Turansky, Scott and Miller, Joanne. *Parenting is Heart Work.* Colorado Springs, CO: Cook Communications, 2006

SUPPORT SERVICES

RESIDENTIAL REHABILITATION PROGRAMS AND OTHER AGENCIES

FREEDOM VILLAGE U.S.A.
5275 Rt. 14
P.O. Box 24
Lakemont, NY 14857
(607) 243-8126
1-800-VICTORY
www.freedomvillageusa.com

FREEDOM VILLAGE CANADA
P.O. Box 1178
Burlington, ON L7R 4L8
(905) 634-5558
1-877-726-5558
www.freedomvillage.ca

TEEN CHALLENGE NETWORK U.S.A.
www.teenchallengeusa.com

TEEN CHALLENGE CANADA
www.teenchallenge.ca

GLOBAL TEEN CHALLENGE
www.globaltc.org

PARENTS—THE ANTI-DRUG
www.theantidrug.com

THE DRUG PREVENTION NETWORK OF CANADA
www.dpnoc.ca

NEW LIFE GIRLS' HOME (CANADA)
www.newlifegirlshome.com

HEARTLIGHT MINISTRIES
www.heartlightministries.org

TO LOCATE OTHER FAITH-BASED SUPPORT SERVICES:
Search the internet using key words such as "Christian teen/youth rehabilitation."

Ask local churches and other related Christian organizations for referrals. Pray for the Holy Spirit's wisdom and discernment, and carefully research each service before making decisions.

Index

Index

Please send us your comments

We would love to hear about the impact this book has had on your life and the difference it has made in your battle for the restoration of a son or daughter or other young people.

- Share your stories with us.
- Let us know about your support/prayer group (if you have started one or already belong to one).
- Let us know if you are interested in connecting with a wider network of Hopekeepers.

Write to: Marva Tyndale
                  Keeping Our Hope Alive
                  Box 29622—377 Burnhamthorpe Road East
                  Mississauga, Ontario L5A 4H2
                  Canada

E-mail us at: info@keepingourhopealive.org

Visit us at: www.keepingourhopealive.org